Telework and Social Change

Telework and Social Change

How Technology Is Reshaping the Boundaries between Home and Work

Nicole B. Ellison

PRAEGER

Westport, Connecticut
London

Library of Congress Cataloging-in-Publication Data

Ellison, Nicole B., 1968–
   Telework and social change : how technology is reshaping the boundaries
between home and work / Nicole B. Ellison.
        p. cm.
   Includes bibliographic̶a̶l̶ ̶r̶e̶f̶e̶r̶e̶n̶c̶e̶s̶ ̶a̶n̶d̶ ̶i̶n̶d̶e̶x̶.
   ISBN 0–275–97800–1̶ ̶(̶a̶l̶k̶.̶ ̶p̶a̶p̶e̶r̶)̶
   1. Telecommuting—S̶o̶c̶i̶a̶l̶ ̶a̶s̶p̶e̶c̶t̶s̶.̶ ̶ ̶2̶.̶ ̶T̶e̶l̶e̶c̶o̶m̶m̶u̶t̶i̶n̶g̶—̶C̶a̶s̶e̶
studies.   I. Title.
   HD2336.3.E38   20̶0̶4̶
   306.3'6—dc22   2̶0̶0̶4̶0̶1̶1̶8̶9̶3̶

British Library Cataloguing in Publication Dat̶a̶ ̶i̶s̶ ̶a̶v̶a̶i̶l̶a̶b̶l̶e̶.̶

Library of Congress Catalog Card Number: 2004011893

ISBN: 0–275–97800–1

First published in 2004

Praeger Publishers, 88 Post Road West, Westport, CT 06881
An imprint of Greenwood Publishing Group, Inc.
www.praeger.com

Printed in the United States of America

∞

The paper used in this book complies with the
Permanent Paper Standard issued by the National
Information Standards Organizations (Z39.48–1984).

10   9   8   7   6   5   4   3   2   1

To My Father,
Gaylord Duane Ellison

Contents

Chapter One

The Social and Organizational Dimensions of Telework

Organizations and individuals are attracted to technology-enabled distributed work for a variety of reasons, including a challenging economic climate, the perceived need to lengthen the workday,[1] globalization trends, and an increase in dual-career families. Individuals, especially women, are drawn to the promise of work/life balance inherent in the notion of working from home. However, the reality of mobile work is often more complicated than either the proponents or the detractors of telework would have us believe. This book explores the adoption of telework at two organizations and the ways in which individuals at these firms used technology to manage the attendant changes in their personal and professional lives.

Telework offers an excellent context in which to study the way information and communication technologies (ICTs) reshape communication patterns in the household and workplace, in part because geographically distributed workers are forced to rely more heavily on mediated communication. Although the percentage of employees who work exclusively at home is relatively small when compared to the number of traditionally structured offices, arrangements in which geographically flexible employees work from multiple locations are rapidly becoming ubiquitous in many industries. Some professions, such as sales, have long relied on heavy travel schedules, but lowered technology costs and greater broadband access have allowed untraditional work arrangements to penetrate other industries as well. Technological advances, economic pressures, and the shifting social landscape have affected organizations in myriad ways, altering the structure and culture of work for organizations, employees, and their households.

This book describes two organizations that adopted telework schemes and focuses on the ways in which telework affected the work and home lives of their employees. Using data collected over a period of 22 months, this study explores the ways in which ICTs triggered changes in work processes, organizational culture, and the social dynamics of the household and family. Based on interviews and observations, this study discusses the way in which employees used communication technologies to encourage and limit the organization's influence on the private sphere of the home. In the home, observations and interviews suggested that the use of communication technologies blurred boundaries between home and work for some teleworkers, but that individuals actively utilized ICTs to calibrate or regulate the permeability of these boundaries—the infiltration of work into their home lives and vice versa. Also, having technologies in the home that promote a high degree of "flow"—technologies such as e-mail and World Wide Web access—occasioned some teleworkers to frequently experience a loss of temporal grounding and a tendency to overwork. In the organizational realm, the adoption of mobile work occasioned changes in management practices, organizational culture, and patterns of socialization and knowledge sharing.

This book explores the ways in which individuals use ICTs to socially shape their home and work environments and to negotiate the many changes that accompany the introduction of "work" into the domestic sphere. The term *social shaping* refers to the ways in which ICTs foreclose or create possibilities rather than "cause" impacts or effects (see MacKenzie & Wajcman, 1985, for a discussion of the term *social shaping of technology*). This study suggests that technologies such as e-mail, cellular phones, and database technology in some cases amplify and reinforce existing trends or tendencies surrounding the separation of home and work boundaries as well as other issues faced by teleworkers, such as the notion of "trust" in telecommuter–supervisor relationships.

In many cases, the movement of paid work into the household encourages individuals to merge formerly distinct roles because the geographical separation between the office and the household has diminished. Innovations in ICTs coupled with changes in job practices have created entire industries in which work is, for the most part, mobile: able to be conducted from homes, cars, clients' offices, airports, hotel rooms. One scholar summarizes this new approach with the following quote, spoken by a vice president of a firm that calls itself a virtual office: work is "something you do, not somewhere you go to" (Handy, 1996, p. 212). However, when work is no longer spatially or temporally bounded to a centralized office, work and nonwork may blend together. Additionally, the lack of a common geographical locus affects the way in which coworkers interact with one another and with support staff and supervisors, demanding dramatic shifts in traditional patterns of communication.

Considering telework as part of the rubric of the "virtual organization" can help us understand some of its implications. Virtual organizations use ICTs to link people and processes that are more geographically distributed than in traditional organizations with a physical center. Although definitions of the term vary, one general definition is that "a 'virtual organization' is composed of private firms or public agencies that have employed ICTs to transform business processes within the organization or among themselves and other organizations" (Dutton, 1996, pp. 4–5). Or, in more extreme terms, "[t]he organization exists, but you can't see it. It is a network, not an office" (Handy, 1996, p. 212). Nohria and Berkley (1994) revisit Max Weber in order to delineate the "organization of the future," taking into consideration the capabilities of technology to manage information and dissolve temporal and geographical boundaries.[2]

Although completely "virtual" organizations may be rare (Kraut, Steinfield, Chan, Butler, & Hoag, 1998), many organizations are exploring various degrees of flexibility regarding the location, time, and definition of work. The number of Americans who work at home, at a telework center or satellite office, or on the road was estimated to be 28 million in 2001 (Davis & Polonko, 2001), and telework increased after the events of September 11, 2001 (Shellenbarger, 2002). In 1998, a survey of facilities managers found that 62 percent of companies were utilizing some form of an alternative workplace strategy, such as telework (La Salle Partners & IFMA, 1998). Not surprisingly, a wave of consulting companies and magazines that specialize in alternative office techniques has followed on the heels of this trend, and even traditional furniture companies like Steelcase are remaking themselves into suppliers for virtual organizations (Fishman, 1996).

Alternative workplace arrangements include telecommuting, job sharing and *flextime*, a term used to describe nontraditional work schedules. In the United States, the term *telecommuting* is generally thought to refer to the completion of paid work in the home, although no standardized definition exists. *Job sharing*, which is attractive to parents and others with time constraints, involves the sharing of one position by two or more employees. *Hoteling* (also called "hot-desking") is often used to refer to employees who work at multiple locations on a regular basis. Instead of having a full-time, dedicated office they use temporary office spaces that are "checked out" for a specific period of time (Hamilton, Baker, & Vlasic, 1996).

Some of these experiments are not entirely successful. For example, the offices of Chiat-Day in Venice, California, one of the earliest adopters of hoteling, were celebrated as an alternative officing success story for their ability to add "$30 million in new billings . . . while cutting [their] real estate holdings by 40 percent" (PS Enterprises, 1995). However, the implementation of Chiat-Day's alternative officing strategy was not without its pitfalls, and in 1997, the company quietly returned to a traditional one-to-one person-to-desk ratio. An article describing this return to traditional organizing quotes Laurie Coots, head of new development at Chiat-Day, as saying "We used to think these were people who just couldn't let go of the past, but we've learned a lot" (Rose, 1997). Coots is the same employee who two years earlier claimed "Work [is] something you do, not somewhere you go to" (Handy, 1996, p. 212).

The company's movement away from hoteling was also described in a scathing article in a popular high-tech industry magazine known for its celebratory attitude toward technology:

> After unburdening all annoying reminders of an actual life, employees headed to the "concierge" window, where they signed out a PowerBook, and the "store," where they were given a programmable portable phone. These tools were on loan only for the day; like members of a kibbutz, Chiat's virtual citizens had little they could call their own—no speed-dial, no hard drive, and, most unsettling of all, no destination point in the wide-open plains of the office. (Berger, 1999)

The article describes the loss of productivity engendered by the organizational scheme, as employees created "work-arounds" to counter the effects of poor design. They sabotaged the concierge system by refusing to return equipment, they stored files in cars and in hiding places around the office, and they tried to commandeer project rooms and turn them into offices. Senior people ordered their lower level assistants to arrive at 6:00 A.M. to claim equipment and a desk. Ironically, the new office space adopted by the company mimics a homey neighborhood, complete with basketball court and park. As Berger (1999) explains, "If the message sent to employees by the virtual office was, 'Get your assignment and hit the road,' this one is saying something entirely different: Stay a while. Stay all night. Hell, you can live here. Which makes obvious sense in a business that is fueled by twentysomethings pulling late-nighters."

Through experiments like the aforementioned, it is clear that despite setbacks and retreats, traditional organizing practices are being revamped. Such new patterns of work are blurring the borders between work and home as organizations increasingly provide employees with amenities such as coffee, meals, social activities and interaction, on-site day care, and even housing (Grimsley, 1998).[3] Increasingly, ICTs have changed communication in the workplace and the household. The use of company-provided pagers and cell phones, for instance, has encouraged a culture of instant and ubiquitous accessibility to work, even during time traditionally reserved for leisure (Brooks, 1998).

OVERVIEW OF THIS BOOK

This book explores the implications of telework, in which communication technologies have blurred many of the traditional borders between home and work, at multiple levels. For individuals, ICTs provide a site for innovation, a means by which employees can creatively negotiate work and family demands and actively calibrate the permeability of their home/work boundaries. For organizations, ICTs can reshape organizational culture, generally defined as the "deeper level of *basic assumptions* and *beliefs* that are shared by members of an organization . . . and that define . . . an organization's view of itself and its environment" (Schein, 1985, p. 6, emphasis in original).

This book uses case studies of two organizations to develop an understanding of the impacts of telework on both the organization and the household. In each of these contexts, the cases highlight interactions among changes in technology, geography, culture, and structure. The use of ICTs triggered changes in work processes, organizational culture, and the culture of the household and family. But these cases also show that the meaning and use of these technologies was mediated, reshaped, and reinterpreted by individuals. One theoretical and practical implication of this story is that it is not useful to focus exclusively on technologically deterministic or socially deterministic approaches to theorizing about the impacts of technology. The outcomes of any given situation depend on the interplay between contextual, historical, and other social variables as well as the changes introduced by technology.

Although telework provides the specific context, this study is more specifically an investigation of the social shaping and impacts of ICTs. As more communication is conducted via ICTs, questions about their impact on our changing communication norms will become more salient.[4] Mediated communication increasingly replaces face-to-face interaction in our day-to-day lives for both interpersonal and organizational communication. This is particularly true for members of dispersed work teams, members of global organizations, and teleworkers. Therefore, these individuals are especially useful to observe if we are to understand and explore some of the implications of the use of new technologies for interpersonal and organizational communication.

Telework research is uniquely suited for exploring changes accompanying our increased use of mediated communication. As an academic area of inquiry, it draws on knowledge from several disciplines and methodologies, depending on the focus of the research and the level of the analysis. For example, telework research has addressed the psychological (Zedeck & Mosier, 1990), organizational (Hamilton, 1987), and societal (Nilles, 1991) impacts of telework. At each of these levels, the movement of paid work from a central location to the household or mobile work space has significant social and cultural implications. Research that addresses the ways in which telework impacts the family or household unit, the organization, and the community will increase our understanding of the role of technology in the workplace and the household. In doing so, the problems and benefits associated with new organizational forms like the virtual organization can be better understood.

These case studies allow us to explore the effects of telework and ICTs at two levels: the home and the organization. At the level of the organization, we can examine the impact of the lack of a central office on organizational culture, the implications of bringing paid work into the household, and the role ICTs play in these changes. This book examines the impact of the lack of a central office on management and supervisory practices, the transfer of organizational knowledge, and teleworkers' access to information in digital and analog form. Because bringing paid work into the household eradicates traditional geographical cues separating "work" from "home," this book will also explore the impact of telework on the household and family structure. Based on interviews and observations, this study will discuss the ways in which employees use communication technologies to encourage and limit the organization's influence on the private sphere of the home. How does telework impact the geography of the household? How do individuals use ICTs to reshape access to work in the household and to shape family members' access to work? How does telework affect the culture of the family, if at all?

Before discussing the case studies in detail, I will briefly summarize some of the ways in which scholars have approached the question of how technology interacts with organizations and society. These three approaches will be helpful to keep in mind throughout the discussion of the case studies.

THE STUDY OF TECHNOLOGY IN ORGANIZATIONS AND SOCIETY

There are three distinct theoretical approaches to the study of technology: technologically deterministic approaches, socially deterministic approaches, and social shaping approaches. These are not theories per se but rather schools of thought that rely on a certain perspective when attempting to explain the interaction between technology and society. In general terms, technologically deterministic theories mark much of the early work on the subject; researchers operating in this vein tend to rely on the characteristics of various technologies in order to explain impact and use. Socially deterministic perspectives focus on social factors to explain changes accompanying the use of technology. A third body of research adopts a broad theoretical perspective that addresses the entire range of design and use, examining the ways technologies are socially shaped.

TECHNOLOGICALLY DETERMINISTIC APPROACHES

Technological determinism can refer to either a general attitude about the ability of technology to "impact" society or this same approach codified in social science theory. In its simplest form, technologically deterministic approaches focus on the introduction of new technologies and their use to explain social change. As MacKenzie and Wajcman (1985) write, "[T]he first part of technological determinism is that technical change is in some sense *autonomous*, 'outside' of society, literally or metaphorically. The second part is that technical change *causes* social change" (pp. 4–5, emphasis in original). For instance, Toffler's work characterizes shifts in the organization of society as being driven by technological change (see Kling, 1996, p. 48).

Cultural approaches to technology that adopt a technologically deterministic standpoint typically take either a Utopian or Dystopian perspective (Kling, 1996). For instance, technology in the workplace is portrayed as either liberating, allowing human beings to concentrate on more fulfilling, cleaner work, or as deskilling, leading to fragmentation and alienation (Braverman, 1985; Webster, 1996). Telework is subject to similar Utopian and Dystopian predictions; it is treated as either a liberating and empowering return to the era of the craftsperson, or as the means by which individual laborers are deskilled and denied a sense of collective unity, essentially turning homes into "electronic sweatshops." Both of these visions are technologically deterministic in that they assume that the technology of telework will have certain impacts regardless of how the technology is designed and employed, and whatever the context.

Theoretical and popular notions adopting this perspective typically do not consider context; the laboratory environment in which much of this research takes place is testament to its failure to consider the social environment. An exemplar of this approach is early research on e-mail that predicted that it would have a decentralizing effect on organizations, because it enabled anyone on the network to send a message to anyone else, bypassing organizational filters like secretaries who screen calls. Other work discussed the democratizing aspects of computer-mediated communication (Sproull & Kiesler, 1991).[5]

Messages that traveled unregulated from office peons to vice presidents would "flatten" the organization's hierarchy, it was argued. Later research on the subject (Schmitz & Fulk, 1991) acknowledged that merely sending an e-mail message was no guarantee that the message would be opened or considered; it might be returned with a note saying "We don't do this around here—talk to your supervisor" (Schmitz & Fulk, 1991, p. 515). In other cases, e-mail filtering software may prevent the message from even being downloaded.

In addition to being a diffuse philosophical perspective, two closely related theories in this genre have been especially generative: social presence theory and media richness theory. Generally, early work in this vein assessed each medium according to its technical attributes. Based on the number of channels through which information was transmitted, media were conceptualized as having various effects on communication or as being more appropriate for certain communicative acts.

Social Presence Theory

Social presence theory graphed media on a spectrum of social presence, which was based on qualities such as "the capacity to transmit information about facial expression, direction of looking, posture, dress and non-verbal vocal cues" (Short, Williams & Christie, 1976, p. 65). *Social Presence* is defined as the "degree of salience of the other person in the interaction and the consequent salience of the interpersonal relationships" (Short, Williams, & Christie, 1976, p. 65). Short, Williams, and Christie (1976) "hypothesize that the users of any given communications medium are in some sense aware of the degree of Social Presence of the medium and tend to avoid using the medium for certain types of interactions" (p. 65). Essentially, research conducted from this perspective looks at the type of communicative information transmitted by a specific medium and argues that some media may be better suited for certain types of communicative action. More ambiguous tasks will require media with more social presence, for example.

This theory has often been overly simplified, represented as if it treated social presence as an objective quality of the medium, although this is inconsistent with the original text. The authors clarify the fact that they "conceive of Social Presence not as an objective quality of the medium, though it must surely be dependent upon the medium's objective qualities, but as a subjective quality of the medium. We believe that this is a more useful way of looking at Social Presence than trying to define it objectively" (p. 66). At any rate, it is clear that the search for explanatory variables is focused on the technology, not the context, users, or other social factors.

Media Richness Theory

Media richness theory (Daft & Lengel, 1986; Trevino, Daft, & Lengel, 1990) also attempts to match tasks with media, based on the "richness" of the medium. Richness is based on four criteria: the availability of instant feedback, the capacity of the medium to transmit multiple cues (such as nonverbals), the use of natural language (as opposed to numbers), and the "*personal focus* of the medium" (Trevino et al., 1990, p. 75, emphasis in original). Weick (1979) suggests that the purpose of organizing is to reduce equivocality—essentially, to gain certainty. Media richness theorists argue that more equivocal tasks should be done face to face, this being the "richest medium," followed by the phone and then e-mail. Unlike social presence theory, which focuses on videoconferencing, media richness theory explicitly considers newer media such as e-mail. However, both of these theories can be critiqued on the grounds that they fail to consider the contextual environment and consider technology as the primary explanatory variable. Both of these approaches, and others in the same vein, privilege face-to-face communication in that it is positioned as the original and true form of communication. Various forms of mediated communication are then evaluated on their ability to replicate face-to-face communication (Contractor & Eisenberg, 1990).

SOCIALLY DETERMINISTIC APPROACHES

Later research shifts the focus from the technology to the user, assuming either individual users or organizations as the critical locus. For example, the Social Influence Model argues that media perceptions are subjective and socially constructed; for instance, through overt statements by coworkers about media characteristics and vicarious learning (Fulk, Schmitz, & Steinfield, 1990). The Social Influence Model predicts that people will vary in how "rich" they perceive a medium to be, but that this variation will not be idiosyncratic. They stress that individuals make decisions that will be invariant but not random, as patterns develop and people start to share realities and interpretations with others in their group. This model elucidates the necessity of considering the social aspects of the use of technology; however, it does not adequately consider the characteristics and design of the technology itself. Additionally, this work fails "to consider influences in the opposite direction; how patterns of media use in turn effect patterns of social interaction and information" (Contractor & Eisenberg, 1990, p. 147).

It should be noted that the question of whether a theory is technologically or socially deterministic depends on which juncture of the technological process the theory examines. Braverman's (1985) deskilling thesis, for example, is socially deterministic at the point of design (technologies are designed to increase managerial control and to disempower the worker by centralizing the locus of control) yet technologically deterministic at the level of the user—the end user has no agency to sabotage or re-create the technology: its impact is predetermined and all encompassing. The Social Influence Model (Schmitz & Fulk, 1991) on the other hand, grants more agency and attention to the user. However, the design and creation of the technology is not considered; technology is assumed to be a black box, not a reflection of the norms or understandings of the creators.

SOCIAL SHAPING APPROACHES

Various areas of research can be categorized within the social shaping of technology approach (Bijker & Law, 1992; MacKenzie & Wajcman, 1985). Generally, these theorists and researchers believe that technologies do not evolve under the impetus of some inner technological or scientific logic, but instead are shaped by many social factors. Many of the researchers that subscribe to this approach focus on the design of technology as well as its use. For instance, Woolgar (1996) argues that technology is "society made durable" (p. 60). These theorists call attention to the factors influencing the development process, which include larger financial and social issues as well as those surrounding the technology itself.[6]

Much of the early work within the social shaping of technology rubric was a reaction to the technologically deterministic bent of early on the subject. This literature can change the way we theorize technology because it makes evident the values embedded in the technology itself. Winner (1994) writes that "one fruitful strategy is to notice how technologies embody ideas. . . . As a person encounters a device or system . . . it is crucial that he or she ask what the form of this thing presupposes about the people who will use it. Having asked that question, one can move on to make explicit what artifact/idea or ideas the object embodies, that is, to give voice to the presuppositions in human-made things" (p. 196).

According to Winner, artifacts do have values. He uses the example of cash registers in a fast-food restaurant, which use pictures of food items instead of words or numbers to announce its theme: "the system is intelligent; its users are not" (p. 197). In explicating the way in which the design of technology is socially shaped, Winner moves us away from assumptions of technologies as neutral or pure, enabling us to acknowledge the social aspects of their creation.

Research on Technology and Structure

Emergent and recursive models of technology's impact on structure and communication can be considered under the rubric of social shaping of technology studies. Although theorists employing these models do not directly reference the aforementioned work and are working in different traditions of research, the general thrust is sympathetic to the social shaping approach because both technological and social characteristics are acknowledged.

For example, the structurational model of technology (Orlikowski, 1992) acknowledges that both the design and use of technology are recursively related.[7] Using a structuration framework (Giddens, 1984), Orlikowski (1992) argues "technology, in conditioning social practices, is both facilitating and constraining. Technology does not only constrain or only enable, but rather does both" (p. 411). Importantly, this work acknowledges that both designers (during the design phase) and users (by sabotage and feedback to designers) can modify technology.

Other important work in this area looks specifically at the relationship between technology and structure (Barley, 1986).[8] Contractor and Eisenberg (1990) argue that perceptions and use of media are the outcome of an interplay among actors, context, and technology and propose the use of communication networks to study the way in which technology use and the social environment shape one another.

Contradictory Findings of Research on Computer-Mediated Communication

Although there is now a substantial body of scholarly work that addresses the relationship between technology and society, gaps still exist. There is a need for more holistic accounts that take into consideration multiple points of interaction with the technology, not just the design or use stages, as well as the characteristics of the technology itself. Research on the ability of computer-mediated communication (CMC) to transmit social and task information and on variables such as productivity has been contradictory. Also, recent research findings are not explained adequately by many of these theories, especially those that take as their focus the objective characteristics of the technology. In many ways, research on CMC has been contradictory and inconclusive (Walther, 1996; Walther, Anderson, & Parks, 1994).

For instance, research that has posited e-mail to be a "thin" medium because of its lack of nonverbal cues argues that CMC is unsuitable for some types of more complex or ambiguous communication (Trevino et al., 1990). However, others have pointed to the fact that users may *exploit* this lack of nonverbals in CMC. Markus (1994/1996) found that e-mail was used more often than any other medium when the relationship between the sender and the receiver involved intimidation or dislike. She argues that "the technological characteristics of e-mail . . . can be perceived by users as a benefit when users do not want personal interaction" (p. 508).

THEORETICAL FOUNDATIONS OF THE STUDY: A SOCIAL SHAPING APPROACH TO TELEWORK

This study suggests that the social shaping perspective is the most appropriate approach for studying the use of ICTs in distributed work environments. It provides the most useful explanation of the way in which organization and household members reshape and adapt technology while also acknowledging the fact that ICTs have an impact on communication.

ICTs have altered existing patterns of communication in the household and organization (Fulk & Steinfield, 1990; Silverstone, 1996; Webster, 1996; Zuboff, 1988). Additionally, ICTs and arrangements such as telework have effectively reshaped organizational duties, relations among family members, and other arenas of interaction. When real change can be attributed to the introduction of telework and the increased use of ICTs, the limits of socially deterministic theories about the use of technology are revealed.

However, differences emerged in the way individuals, organizations, and families negotiated telework and the use of ICTs. For instance, individuals uniquely shaped both the technology and geography of the household to construct boundaries between home and work roles. As traditional cues about where and when work should take place are muted, communication technology tools are increasingly utilized as a way for organization members to regulate the infiltration of work-related influences into the home. Because the use of ICTs and the way telework is introduced into the household vary depending on the organizational and individual context, technologically deterministic arguments concerning telework are neither appropriate nor useful. The social shaping approach clearly offers the richest and most suitable means by which to understand these phenomena, because it acknowledges the importance of studying both the technology and the social environment.

CONTEXT-EMBEDDED RESEARCH ON THE
VIRTUAL ORGANIZATION

As they embrace arrangements like mobile work, hoteling, and telework, many organizations are moving away from traditional workplaces and toward a model of fluidity regarding the location and timing of work. This movement is heralded in many management and popular press accounts as a liberating and empowering shift for both organizations and individual employees. Advertising companies have contributed to stereotyped notions of telecommuters as slipper-wearing, unshowered parents who care for children while teleconferencing with clients, bragging all the while about their productivity and newfound freedom (Shellenbarger, 1997b).

More nuanced and accurate descriptions that capture the complexities of telework may be best revealed through in-depth interviews and case studies. In the late 1980s, author Tom Forester (1988/1989) wrote about his own experiences working at home, marked by isolation and loneliness, and proposed that most of the telework literature was written by people who had not worked at home and therefore had little understanding of the problems it entailed. More recent telework research may be subject to the same critique. Although more qualitative work has attempted to convey a more nuanced portrayal of telework, in many cases the rhetoric of telework and the virtual organization is simplistically Utopian.

In many popular press and academic accounts, the notion of the virtual organization serves as a sort of rhetorical ideal that promises to be a panacea for all the problems associated with traditional modes of organizing. Therefore, many discussions of virtual organizations are based on idealized prototypes that are not grounded in real-life experiences and situations. As Fulk, Schmitz, and Schwarz (1992) write, "Until we can capture the complexity of both the social context and its interaction with communication behavior, our knowledge claims will remain limited" (p. 7). This study attempts to provide a contextual, grounded description of the changing communicative processes associated with these new organizational forms.

THE ORGANIZATIONS:
iLAN SYSTEMS AND XYZ

This book is based on research conducted at two technology-oriented organizations located in Southern California, iLAN Systems and XYZ.[9] Both organizations employed several teleworkers, known as "cybercommuters" and "mobile workers" at XYZ.[10] Case studies on iLAN Systems and XYZ were initiated in late 1996 and early 1997 for inclusion in a research report on the subject of virtual organizations. These organizations were selected because they exemplified qualities of innovativeness and the use of ICTs to reshape traditional geographical and functional patterns. This book extends and elaborates on this initial research.

iLAN Systems and XYZ have unique characteristics that make them useful to study. Both organizations had adopted mobile work styles, used ICTs extensively, and were in the technology industry. However, they also differed in key aspects. One important distinction hinged on the fact that iLAN Systems was created as a virtual firm whereas XYZ adopted telework after a traditional work style was already established as part of the organizational culture. Because this shift occurred during the course of the study, it was possible to get a keen sense of how these changes affected the individuals at XYZ, who were able to articulate differences between the new system, which they had not yet grown used to, and the old system, which was still fresh in their memory and experience.

STRUCTURE OF THIS BOOK

This book uses case studies of two organizations to develop an understanding of the ways in which technologies are used by teleworkers in both the organization and the household. Using data collected over a period of 22 months (primarily in 1998 and 1999), this study explores the ways in which ICTs triggered changes in work processes, organizational culture, and the culture of the household and family. Chapter 2 summarizes what we know about telework and telecommuting arrangements, based on research in the fields of communication, sociology, business, architecture, transportation, urban studies, and technology studies. This chapter also discusses some of the definitional issues that have plagued the study of telework and some of the primary reasons telework adoption rates have not met early expectations.

Chapter 3 will cover the iLAN Systems case study, describing the organization's culture and history, and Chapter 4 discusses the XYZ case study, focusing on the shift from a traditional workplace to mobile work. Addressing the impact of telework at the level of the organization, Chapter 5 examines how the lack of a central office affected management and supervisory practices, the transfer of organizational knowledge, and teleworkers' access to information in digital and analog form. Chapter 6 focuses on the household and suggests that the use of communication technologies in the home blurred boundaries between home and work for some teleworkers, but that individuals actively utilized ICTs to calibrate the permeability of these boundaries—the infiltration of work into their home lives and vice versa. Also, having technologies in the home that promote a high degree of "flow" (Csikszentmihalyi, 1990)—technologies such as e-mail and World Wide Web access—occasioned some teleworkers to frequently experience a loss of temporal grounding and a tendency to overwork. The concluding chapter summarizes the findings and makes suggestions for future research in this area.

Chapter Two
What We Know about Telework

This chapter will review some of what we already know about telework and its effects on individuals, organizations, and families. Much of the literature on telework, especially from the managerial perspective, examines the question of how to manage nonvisible (remote) workers. Other research has examined how organizational knowledge can be transmitted and organizational cultures maintained in a telecommuting environment, where workers may be physically isolated from their colleagues. Another large body of telework research looks at role construction and the way in which telework blurs the boundaries between "home" and "work."

One of the most important things to realize about the research on telework (also called "home-based work" or "telecommuting") is that it is fragmented, hindered primarily by the fact that practitioners, consultants, and scholars all subscribe to different definitions of telework, telecommuting, mobile work, and so on. There is little consensus concerning who should be classified as a teleworker or telecommuter, although there have been attempts at creating organizational schemes that classify different types of telework and telecommuting arrangements (Fritz, Higa, & Narasimhan, 1995; Manley & Tolbert, 1997; Mokhtarian, 1991a).

When the term *telecommuting* was originally coined, it referred specifically to the use of communication and information technologies to replace transportation (Nilles, Carlson, Gray, & Hanneman, 1976). It is not uncommon to see the terms *telework* and *telecommuting* used almost interchangeably; *telework* is used more often in Europe whereas *telecommuting* is more popular in the

United States. Others distinguish between the two; for instance, Nilles (1998) defines *teleworking* as "ANY form of substitution of information technologies for work-related travel" but *telecommuting* more specifically as "periodic work out of the principal office, one or more days per week either at home, a client's site, or in a telework center" (p. 1).

Throughout this book I use *telework* more broadly to refer to work done outside a central office in which employees are co-located and *telecommuting* or *work at home* as a subset of *telework*, referring more specifically to work done in the home. This terminology differs slightly from that used by Nilles (1997), who defines *teleworking* as "the use of information technology to partially or totally replace work-related travel" and *telecommuting* as "that part of teleworking associated with the daily commute between employees' homes and their principle workplaces" (p. 7).

Among researchers there is some disagreement about whether *telework* and *telecommuting* should apply to *any* work done in the home, or just work that relies on the use of information and communication technologies. Some researchers (e.g., Cross & Raizman, 1986) see these terms as containing an emphasis on communications technology and in fact may explicitly include technology in their definition of *telecommuting* whereas other definitions of *telecommuting* contain no reference whatsoever to technology or telecommunications.[1] Early work on the subject stressed that technology was not a driving force of telework (Olson, 1988b), but more recently, "road warriors" consider their technological devices a crucial component of their departure from the central office (Takahashi, 1996).

My personal approach is to consider all types of work conducted outside a centrally located work space (including work done in the home) as telework, but to reserve *telecommuting* to refer more specifically to work done in the home, whether it is facilitated through broadband connection and a computer or by phone lines or by pen and paper. If one embraces a wide and fluid definition of technology—such as that which extends the power of the human body—then there is very little work that does not involve some type of technology, however rudimentary. That said, in this study I focus on individuals who do rely heavily on information and communication technologies in the hopes of learning how their use of information and communications technologies affect their experience of working outside a centrally located workplace.

Although in recent years some exciting work has been done on the topic, a significant proportion of the scholarly research on telecommuting and telework was conducted in the late 1970s and 1980s, before the explosion of the Internet and the introduction of relatively inexpensive ICTs such as handheld wireless devices and cellular phones. These technologies, which have reconfigured access to information, people, services, and technology (Dutton, 1999), have significantly affected the communicative strategies and daily experience of many teleworkers. Therefore, the extent to which some of this early research on telecommuting is applicable to today's communicative environment is unclear.

The large and growing body of research on telework, which spans many academic disciplines and is authored by practitioners as well as academics, has many foci. For instance, organizational communication scholars are concerned primarily with scenarios in which supervisors and coworkers are not co-located, whereas research focusing on the psychological impact of bringing paid work (the "public") into the domestic sphere (the "private") is more specifically concerned with work-at-home situations. In summarizing the work on this topic, I will focus on research most applicable to the issues at hand: the effects of telework on the individual and her personal and professional lives, and the ways in which individuals use technology to enhance or mitigate these changes.

Before delving into the body of research on telework, it is useful to consider the history of telework itself. Some researchers argue that home-based work dates back to the Preindustrial Era, when craftspeople and their families labored together in their homes. More recently, however, in the United States, the popularity of telecommuting initially rose during the gas shortages of the 1970s, when long lines for scarce gasoline sparked interest in work arrangements that would eradicate or decrease commutes. In fact the research of Jack Nilles, one of the early authorities on telework, was inspired by the oil embargo of the 1970s. As noted by Huws, Korte, and Robinson (1990) and others, telework research of the early 1970s, which focused on what Nilles and his colleagues called the transportation-technology trade-off (Nilles et al., 1976) was often inspired by the possibility that technology could be used to replace travel to work. The most well-known text in this body of work is the 1976 book by Nilles, Carlson, Gray, and Hanneman, in which the term *telecommuting* was coined. Since this early work, other researchers have continued to examine telework as a possible solution to some of the negative effects that accompany commuting culture, such as automobile emissions and other environmental problems.[2]

In the 1980s, published material on telework consisted of futuristic (and often Utopian) visions of the "electronic cottage" (Toffler, 1980) as well as negative portrayals that exposed the mundane and often lonely reality of telecommuting. For instance, one article in this genre is titled "Working at Home: Is It Freedom or a Life of Flabby Loneliness?" (E. Larson, cited in Huws et. al, 1990, p. xiv). Other publications focused on giving telecommuters prescriptive advice about how to work at home and what to expect (See Huws et al., 1990).

In the past twenty or so years, organizations have explored the concept of the virtual organization and mobile work as strategies by which they might lower real estate and other costs, attract or retain employees, and increase productivity. Research addressing these issues differs from the earlier transportation-technology trade-off literature in that the focus is on disassociating the activity of work from a single, centralized workplace, rather than shifting work specifically to the home environment.

Most teleworkers claim higher productivity levels than when they had a traditional workplace and schedule (Di Martino & Wirth, 1990; Gordon, 1988; Olson, 1988a; Pratt, 1984; Westfall, 1998). However, many of these reports are based on self-reported data and the productivity of knowledge workers is notoriously difficult to assess. Westfall (1998) suggests "at least some of the productivity gains from telecommuting are based on exaggerated self-evaluations" (p. 261). Ironically, employees whose productivity is easily measured, such as clerical workers, are less likely to be given the opportunity to telecommute than are knowledge workers (Guthrie, 1997). Additionally, the validity of self-reported productivity scores is suspect. After all, if one wants to continue working from home, reporting decreased productivity is not the best way to ensure this. Among the many reasons cited for the increase in productivity among teleworkers are saved commute time (which usually translates into more time spent working), less disruptions and interruptions, and more harmony between the employee's "biological clock" and when he or she works. In addition, other factors include faster processing time (when teleworkers access the Internet or mainframe computers during off-peak hours) and less incidental absence (Gordon, 1988). Nilles (1997) claims that not only do individual teleworkers become more productive, but their fellow, nonteleworking colleagues do as well. This is attributed in part to the fact that teleworking employees become more self-reliant problem solvers, which allows others back at the office to focus on their formally assigned tasks.

The more recent, renewed focus on telework has been prompted in large part by the introduction of new technologies, which increase the speed and quality of coordination while reducing its costs (Malone & Rockart, 1991). We also know more about the ways in which computer-mediated communication is used in organizations (Contractor & Eisenberg, 1990; Fulk, Schmitz & Steinfield, 1990; Lievrouw & Livingstone, 2002; Schmitz & Fulk, 1991) and to initiate friendships and romantic relationships (Lea & Spears, 1995; McLaughlin, Osbourne & Ellison, 1997; Parks & Floyd, 1996; Rice & Love, 1987; Walther, 1992; Walther, Anderson, & Park, 1994). In general, this body of literature seems to suggest that the Internet is, for many, a positive social venue that is integrated into their daily lives and experiences. As broadband technologies become more common and ICTs less expensive, teleworkers will have increased access to new tools for managing work and social relationships. However, it is difficult to predict how these tools will be used by teleworkers, their colleagues, and their managers.

TELEWORKERS: WHO AND HOW MANY?

As suggested earlier, the accuracy of many of the calculations regarding teleworkers, both in the United States and globally, is undetermined, due in large part to differing definitions and methodologies (Kraut, 1987, 1988; Qvortrup, 1998; Shafizadeh, Niemeier, Mokhtarian, & Salomon, 1997). One researcher likened the counting of teleworkers to "measuring a rubber band. The result depends on how far you stretch your definition" (Qvortrup, 1998, p. 21) and others write about the "tortuous and disputed route of trying to establish a clear definition of telework" (McGrath & Houlihan, 1998, p. 58).

Quantitative studies of telework tend to focus on attempts to chart the current extent of the phenomenon and its potential future growth (Jackson & van der Wielen, 1998). The vast range of definitions, methodologies, and calculation strategies has resulted in estimates of telework adoption that differ greatly, making it difficult to compare data from different studies (Huws et al., 1990; Jackson & van der Wielen, 1998) or to monitor telework for policy purposes (Mokhtarian, 1991a). Also, many of the organizations and individuals that fund and conduct these telework studies have a vested interest in the findings, which may affect the criteria they adopt and therefore their results (Jackson & van der Wielen, 1998).[3] Given the lack of definitional consensus, it is not surprising that estimates of telework are likely to differ by as much as a factor of 10 (Parliamentary Office of Science and Technology, 1995). Unresolved definitional issues include questions about how to categorize "moonlighters" (those who work at home as a second job), individuals who complete insignificant paid work at home, and employees who work from home but do not use ICTs. Should transportation be considered? (Some researchers do not consider a husband and wife running a home-based business to be telecommuters, because they are not replacing transportation with ICTs.) How do we categorize home-based business owners, those reporting to telecenters (Mokhtarian, 1991b), and mobile workers who work neither at home nor at a central office? These questions remain unresolved. One example of the extent to which numbers can vary is that estimates of the number of telecommuters in the United States in 1997 ranged from 9 million to 42 million (Wells, 1997). IDC/Link, a technology research company, estimated the number of work-at-home households in 1997 to be 32.7 million (Wells, 1997) but the Bureau of Labor Statistics reported that "more than 21 million persons did some work at home as part of their primary job in May 1997" (U.S. Department of Labor, 1998); however of these 21 million individuals, more than 11 million were bringing work home from the office. So, for instance, this figure includes cases such as an elementary school teacher creating a lesson plan over coffee in her kitchen. To complicate matters further, as the president of the Institute for the Study of Distributed Work notes, "no one has done a complete and large-enough random sample of U.S. residences to really find out what's going on out there" (Wells, 1997). So, even if one definition does become universally accepted, a large data collection effort would still have to take place before we know the true extent of this phenomena in the United States and globally.

More recent domestic figures estimate the number of Americans who work at home, at a telework center or satellite office, or "on the road" to be 28 million (Davis & Polonko, 2001). According to the International Telework Association and Council, about 20 percent of the adult workforce in the United States does some type of telework (Davis & Polonko, 2001). IDC, a U.S. technology research firm, predicts that the number of mobile workers in the United States will increase from 92 million in 2001 to 105 million in 2006 and, that by the end of 2006, roughly two-thirds of U.S. workers will be mobile workers (IDC, 2002). One recent study suggests that telework may be more attractive to individuals and organizations in the post–September 11 climate: since then, telework has increased at a rate of 3 percent annually (Shellenbarger, 2002). The European Commission, using a fairly broad definition that includes use of ICTs, reported 9 million teleworkers in Europe in 1999, 75 percent of whom were male (European Commission, 2000).

In the United States, California in particular enjoys a large number of both telecommuters and telework researchers (see, e.g., Mokhtarian, 1991b; Nilles, 1991; PS Enterprises, 1995), which is ironic given the well-documented affair Los Angeles has with the automobile (Brodsly, 1981). Jack Nilles, "the father of telecommuting," resides in Los Angeles, and Southern California is the focus of much of his research (Nilles, 1991; Nilles et al., 1976). Also, California's air quality regulations (Mokhtarian, 1991b; Park, Nilles, & Baer, 1996), natural disasters (such as earthquakes), and geographical dispersion make it a natural environment for telecomuting experimentation.[4]

MANAGEMENT OF TELEWORKERS: SUPERVISION, TRUST, AND PRODUCTIVITY

Despite the increased productivity attributed to telework and the obvious benefits to the environment, the number of teleworkers in the United States is still much lower than was predicted during the first wave of telework research. In 1971, AT&T forecasted that by 1990 the *entire* U.S. labor force would be working from home (Steinle, 1988)—and this is only one example of the optimistic predictions concerning telework. The chief reason telework has not met these early predictions is that many organizations are uncomfortable with the lack of visibility and control entailed by off-site workers (Bailyn, 1989; Cross & Raizman, 1986; Gordon & Kelly, 1986; Olson, 1988a, 1988b, 1989). The new evaluation strategies needed for teleworking employees may be unattractive to managers, who must shift from a behavior-based evaluation system ("Is Joe at his desk?") to an outcome-based system ("Has Joe completed X, Y, and Z?"), and risky for employees (Westfall, 1997). Managers who have relied on visual cues to assess performance might find it difficult, time-consuming, or just irritating to shift to a "manage-by-results" paradigm.

Researchers have explored the reasons some managers have resisted adopting telework. In addition to the loss of power entailed by sending workers off-site, in some cases resistance to telework is rooted in long-held beliefs about the appropriate location and structure of work. Kraut (1987) argues that the traditional office environment is a legacy of the factory system and industrialization, and that telework violates established organizational and personal norms such as those that dictate the separation of home and work activities. Gordon (1988) notes that close supervision of direct work was originally a crucial component of factory labor; although our work locale has shifted dramatically, our supervisory habits have not.

Over 15 years ago Gordon (1988) wrote that "fear of loss of control" is "perhaps the biggest reason why telecommuting is showing slower progress than some had expected" (p. 121). Today, managerial resistance to off-site employees is still a factor for those organizations who do not allow their employees to telework, as indicated by the many articles on managing telecommuters that stress the importance of shifting from observation of activity to objective assessment of output quality (e.g. Abreu, 2000; Pancucci, 1995). In one review of the telework literature, almost all the articles written for managers emphasized the need to develop "new management styles" (Huws, Korte, & Robinson, 1990, p. 29). Olson (1989) found that managers felt that supervising teleworkers meant more time spent working—time they did not feel was "particularly beneficial even if it resulted in better planning and time estimates" (p. 334). Organizational norms about visibility are deeply ingrained. In fact, some research suggests that it is more difficult for teleworkers to receive raises or promotions (Hamilton, 1987; Harpaz, 2002; Olson, 1988a; Perin, 1991), which are linked in some organizations to an employee's visibility.

TRUST IN THE TELEWORK ENVIRONMENT

The concept of trust appears often in the telework research, most often as a vaguely articulated yet critical aspect of off-site managerial relationships. Handy (1995) asks, "How do you manage people whom you do not see? The simple answer is, By trusting them, but the apparent simplicity disguises a turnaround in organizational thinking" (p. 41). Much of the telework literature assumes that trust is a vital prerequisite for work that occurs off-site and without direct supervision.

However, in some cases the shift to telework is accompanied by a greater demand for complex documentation and training (A. Lallande, as cited in Huws et al., 1990). This response requires teleworkers to complete time-consuming documentation, which paradoxically eliminates any productivity gains engendered by telework. This dynamic illustrates the central problem with traditional management styles, in which supervisors manage by "observing activity" (Gordon, 1988) or "by walking around" (J. Nilles, quoted in Johnson, 1997, p. 90). In this environment, employees are effectively conditioned to "look busy." As Gordon and Kelly (1986) note, "whether they're actually doing anything of value is another story" (p. 74). This tendency is evidenced by the inclusion of "boss buttons" in some video games—icons that trigger a fake spreadsheet to quickly fill the screen for the benefit of passing managers.

In one of the few research studies specifically examining the relationship between teleworkers and their managers, Reinsch (1997) suggests that these relationships may deteriorate after an initially positive honeymoon phase and calls for more longitudinal research on the subject. Kurland and Egan (1999), who look at the relationship between telecommuting, monitoring strategies, and organizational justice perceptions, suggest that telecommuters generally perceive themselves to be treated fairly. They also note that many organizations are not adopting changes in managerial practice, such as focusing on objective criteria. Harrington and Ruppel (1999) find that managers are more likely to embrace telecommuting arrangements if they trust their employees and note that this trust is a function of the organizational culture. That is, some cultures are more suited to the high levels of trust telecommuting might seem to demand due to their focus on group values and rational performance-based appraisals.

It is clear that if telework is to be adopted on a massive scale, a paradigm shift of managerial norms and attitudes will need to precede it. In the meantime, technological surveillance might assuage some concerns. For example, videoconferencing can mimic line-of-sight supervision of distant employees. Interestingly, Symantec introduced a piece of software created specifically for telecommuters called "pcTelecommute." Although it performs valuable functions like version control of files, descriptions of the software boast that it "automatically logs all incoming and dial-assisted outgoing calls, sent and received faxes, and file changes. Just format the status report using the included Microsoft Word template and it's ready to give to your manager" (Symantec, n.d.). So while prescriptive texts might stress the importance of managing by objectives, software "designed for and by telecommuters" logs each call, file alteration, and file transfer, in preparation for lengthy reports detailing each moment of productivity or lack thereof.

Regardless of how or whether telework has been adopted, the very concept of telework has functioned to make organizational norms and practices more evident and has helped bring questions about managerial reliance on line-of-sight supervision into the open. As one article on the subject observes, "[T]elework does not call for more trust; it calls for careful assessment and reapplication of the trust that is necessary for organisational [sic] performance in the first place" (T. Miller, cited in Huws et al., 1990, p. 31).

ORGANIZATIONAL CULTURE AND EMPLOYEE ISOLATION

Understanding an organization's culture is an important part of understanding how the organization functions, what it means to its employees, and a host of other items. Sometimes conceptualized as the glue that binds individual employees into a more cohesive group, an organization's culture, or cultures, emerge from the perceptions, beliefs, values, memories, and experiences of the members (Martin, 1992, p. 3). Some argue that culture is an intrinsic component of organizations rather than an extrinsic influence (Smircich & Calas, 1987). Because organizational culture is communicatively constructed, researchers do not limit their observations to formal communication like speeches and mottos, but also consider everyday conversations and mundane details (Barley, 1983/1991; Eisenberg & Riley, 2001). Using a cultural lens, Hylmö and Buzzanell (2002) explore some of the paradoxes encountered by telecommuters and make pragmatic suggestions about ways in which organizations could help telecommuters and those at the office better understand and legitimize what it means to be a telecommuter. It is clear that the culture of an organization is an important determinant of whether teleworkers feel isolated or connected, supported or shunned.

Olson (1988a, 1988b), who has studied the role of organizational culture in determining the adoption of telework, notes, "The one overlooked social force which is and will continue to be a major barrier to telework is organizational culture, and in particular management style. . . . Furthermore, organizational culture dictates a commitment to the organization as a place. . . . In all respects, the notion of an employee working at home when and where he or she wants flies in the face of this corporate culture (1988b, pp. 97–98). Although Olson is speaking to a generalized notion of traditional corporate norms rather than to a specific organizational environment as considered by the organizational communication literature, her point is salient and, in many cases, still valid. For instance, a 1995 survey of facilities managers found that they reported organizational culture to be the primary barrier to the adoption of alternative office arrangements (International Facility Management Association & Haworth, 1995).

ISOLATION OF TELEWORKERS AND THE SOCIAL ASPECTS OF THE OFFICE

Telework is often associated with isolation (both expected and actual) and this has been a key factor in the limited adoption of distributed work (Forester, 1988/1989; Olson 1988b; Pratt, 1984). In fact, there are even products that attempt to fill the silence of an empty house with comforting sounds of keyboards clicking and the like: "Office Chatter/Computer Chatter," is described as "audiotapes of actual office sounds to play in the home office to give the feeling of being in the corporate office" (Switzer, 1997, p. 147). Social networking and friendship formation as well as vital informal information dissemination typically take place in the workplace (Sias & Cahill, 1998; Salomon & Salomon, 1984), and those who work at home may also be missing out on the informal perks of working at the office, such as meeting prospective romantic partners. Reporting on his own experience as a teleworker, Forester (1988/1989) writes that, after an initial "honeymoon" period, his telecommuting experience was marked by "feelings of loneliness, isolation, and a growing desire to escape the 'same four walls'" (p. 218) and argues that most of the books and articles celebrating telework are not based on actual experience. Because they are written by people who have not actually experienced telework, he argues, they underestimate the psychological stress telecommuting entails.

Traditional office workers meet social needs at the office through informal channels, which may not be available to those off-site (Forester, 1988/1989; Pratt, 1984). Kraut (1987) attributes the persistence of the traditional office structure to the fact that employees derive social support and satisfaction from social-izing with coworkers and Stohl (1995) notes that "coworkers are not available for social and task support" (p. 9) when employees are not co-located. Informal channels of communication—which are associated with proximity—are important for sharing organi-zational norms, for socializing new employees, and for encourag-ing collaboration (Kraut, 1987; National Research Council, 1994). In addition to missing out on "face time" with supervisors, tele-workers may miss out on other career development opportunities, such as informal networks and mentoring (Hill, 1995) and the stimulation of sharing ideas with coworkers (Hamilton, 1987). Critical organizational knowledge (information about clients, sales strategies, gossip)—has traditionally been shared through spontaneous and informal interactions when employees are co-located (Brown & Duguid, 2000). Teleworkers who work off-site may find it difficult to re-create some of these bonds from afar, al-though instant messaging—a synchronous technology around which informal communication norms have developed—appears to be promising in this respect.

The symbol of the watercooler is often referenced by tele-workers as a way of representing the intangible social aspects of the workplace that are unavailable to those not physically present. Pratt (1984) found that young, single men and women who relied on office networks for social contacts stopped work-ing at home and returned to the office for "standing around the water cooler" socialization (p. 6). However, more recently, a telecommuter told a reporter, "E-mail has become my substi-tute for the water cooler. I look forward to those messages every day" (Ginsberg, 1997).

As this comment suggests, cheaper, faster, and more ubiq-uitous communication tools have the potential to re-create some of the social connections enjoyed by co-located employees. We know that computer-mediated communication is able to convey socioemotional as well as task information and can result in the formation of online communities and social networks (Baym, 1995; McLaughlin et al., 1997; Rheingold, 1993; Rice & Love, 1987). Some research suggests that communication technology use moderates negative feelings about telecommuting and miti-gates fears of isolation (Ramsower, 1985). As the capabilities and availability of communication tools continues to improve, it is conceivable that the actual or expected isolation feared by tele-workers might be mitigated. For instance, although Sias and Cahill (1998) link physical proximity to friendship formation in workplaces and suggest that telecommuting may entail "significant costs to human relationships" (p. 291), they also note that ICTs may serve as a substitute for proximity in some situations.

It is unlikely that computer-mediated communication will ever completely replace face-to-face interaction for all social and task-related communication in the office environment. The same qualities that make it more appropriate for some types of communication also make it less desirable for other purposes. For example, some office workers report that office gossip is one of the things they would miss most (Mogelonsky, 1995). Office gossip is also a method by which organizational norms are enforced (Kraut, 1987). However, the documenting properties of e-mail that make it valuable in the work environment (Markus, 1994/1996) would seem to make it unsuitable for gossiping or dissemination of sensitive information, although some research has shown that teleworkers do share grapevine information via e-mail (Scott & Timmerman, 1999). I expect that newer communication technologies that more closely emulate spontaneous, informal communication—such as instant messaging and SMS (Short Message Service)—will be used to share informal information among virtual coworkers to a greater degree in the future.

ORGANIZATIONAL COMMITMENT AND TELEWORK

The effects of telework on organizational identification (which speaks to an employee's level of commitment and attachment to the organization) are unclear. It is generally assumed that telework reduces organizational commitment since off-site employees are less likely to come into contact with organizational symbols and messages, an assumption supported by some research (Olson, 1983, 1989; Olson & Primps, 1990). Conversely, the opportunity to work at home may allow employees to address issues such as child care, making these employees *more* committed to the organization (Bailyn, 1989; Olson & Primps, 1990). Wiesenfeld, Raghuram, and Garud (1998) examined organizational identification among virtual workers and found a strong relationship between electronic communication and organizational identification, which suggests that "electronic media are particularly important to the maintenance of organizational identification" (Wiesenfeld, Raghuram, & Garud, 1998). Scott and Timmerman (1999) examine identification among teleworkers and find that teleworkers who work away from the central office a moderate amount of time (about 50 percent) are more identified than those who telework less often or more often. This may be because those who work away from the office quite frequently are not there enough to identify with the organization and its values, but that those who telework infrequently are not trusted by supervisors or do not have enough flexibility in their work practices, both of which might lower identification. At any rate this study does point out the "chicken and egg" problem with researching the issue of trust within the telework context: the challenge of ascertaining whether telework results in employees becoming more trusted (perhaps because they become more productive) or whether only trusted employees are allowed to work off-site. Additionally, the question of whether electronic communication is suitable for creating organizational identification or just maintaining it remains unclear.

As Olson (1988a) and others have noted, organizations typically express and reflect organizational norms through physical aspects of the organization. Physical artifacts—like decorations and awards, furniture, and office size—serve to maintain organizational culture by strengthening organizational identification (Dutton, Dukerich, & Harquail, 1994) and by indicating employee status and hierarchy. These visual communication devices are unavailable to teleworkers, who may not spend time in a centralized office. From the teleworker's perspective, conformity, acceptance of organizational norms and customs, and predictability are rewarded in bureaucracies, and it is more difficult to demonstrate these qualities while working at home (Olson, 1988a).

ORGANIZATIONAL KNOWLEDGE AND TELEWORK

The transfer of organizational knowledge in distributed work settings is an important area of academic and industry inquiry. According to Nonaka (1994), organizational knowledge can be either explicit (easily codified) or tacit (dynamic and difficult to codify). Understanding the means by which organizational knowledge is shared by dispersed employees has pragmatic value for organizations, especially those in which employees are not co-located. Although ICTs can help organizations organize and distribute codified (explicit) knowledge, these tools (such as databases) are far less useful when managing tacit knowledge. In one of the few pieces to specifically examine the transfer of organizational knowledge among teleworkers, Raghuram (1996) notes that telework may hamper the creation and transfer of tacit knowledge and suggests strategies like the use of mentors, face-to-face meetings, and rotation of teleworkers to encourage the sharing of tacit knowledge. More work needs to be done to conceptualize ways in which knowledge and information can be shared among members of a distributed work team, especially unstructured knowledge (National Research Council, 1994, p. 61).

BOUNDARIES BETWEEN HOME AND WORK

Telework disrupts traditional distinctions between home and work—two concepts traditionally placed in binary opposition to one another. Industrialization and the centralization of the workplace helped create the "notion of work and family as separate and relatively autonomous behavioral spheres" (Christensen, 1988b, p. 2). The home traditionally is associated with private life: familial relations, women, unpaid labor, and domesticity (Rawlins, 1998). Telework blurs these distinctions between home and work and inserts public work life back into the private sphere of the home. Although much of the literature on new forms of organizing focuses on the impact of work leaving the workplace, the other half of the story is just as important: where does that work go once it leaves the office? And what happens there?

Also called "virtual organizations" (Chesbrough & Teece, 1996; Davidow & Malone, 1992; Nohria & Berkley, 1994) or "networked organizations" (Sproull & Kiesler, 1991), boundaryless organizations capitalize on the fact that knowledge work is not location-bound or temporally constrained.[5] Organizations and teams can be pulled together for the extent of a project and then disbanded—contract laborers hired "just in time" to meet production demands and then dismissed—and global work teams can hand off files as their workday ends, effectively creating an extended workday as projects follow daylight across the globe (Gilhooly, 2001).

A primary focus of telework researchers has been the question of how teleworkers adjust to the blurring of boundaries between "home" and "work" (Beach, 1989; Duxbury, Higgins, & Mills, 1992; Hill, Hawkins, & Miller, 1996; Nippert-Eng, 1996). Indeed, in recent times our traditional concepts of home and work may be replacing one another in that home is chaotic, a place (especially for women) in which there is always too much to do and not enough time to do it in, whereas in the workplace adults feel in control, rewarded, and able to socialize (Hochschild, 1997).[6]

Today's communication technologies such as home fax machines, cell phones, and pagers enable the domestic and professional realms to bleed into one another in new and ubiquitous ways. The traditional office environment aids workers in structuring their time and attention. Alternative work arrangements, like telecommuting, dismantle temporal and geographical barriers that separate home and work roles, exposing employees to the possibility of role conflict (Kraut, 1987, pp. 131–132). In the past, individuals have identified geographical locales with various roles or aspects of their identity. For instance, a man might identify himself as Catholic, a father, and a lawyer, but each of these roles will be more salient in the church, the home, and the courthouse. When the home is the locus for all the professional and personal aspects of our identity, we receive conflicting cues about who we should be when. *Role conflict* (the occurrence of simultaneous, conflicting demands) and *role ambiguity* (the lack of information about expectations concerning role performance) have been examined in relation to telework (Olson, 1989; Shamir & Salomon, 1985). It is suggested that that women will experience more role conflict while telecommuting then men (Shamir & Solomon, 1985) and there appears to be little consensus about whether working at home definitively has either a positive or a negative impact in regard to work–family relations (Shamir, 1992).

Of particular interest to telework researchers are the transitions between the domains of "home" and "work" and the means by which the boundaries between them are negotiated. Nippert-Eng (1996) calls this "boundary work": the "process through which we organize potentially realm-specific matters, people, objects, and aspects of the self into 'home' and 'work'" (p. 7). The commute to and from work has traditionally existed as a structured space for the transition from one role to another (Hall, 1990; Hall & Richter, 1988; Salomon & Salomon, 1984), in that the physical movement helps induce our "mental movement between realms" (Nippert-Eng, 1996, p. 110). In fact, in one study, 60 percent of the respondents agreed that "commuting is a useful interlude between home and work" (Nilles et al., 1976). The need for some kind of distance (geographical and therefore temporal) between home and work is suggested (Salomon & Salomon, 1984). For instance, commuting is said to be desirable because it gave respondents "time for being by themselves" (C. Delesalle & D. Poggi, cited in Salomon & Salomon, 1984, p. 24).

Many teleworkers create other kinds of boundaries to replace the geographical distance traditional work arrangements provide (Ahrentzen, 1990; Kompast & Wagner, 1998; Smith, 1996). For example, some teleworkers wear a specific piece of clothing to indicate that they are "working" (Davies, n.d.) and over half of the teleworkers interviewed for Ahrentzen's (1990) study performed a ritual that marked the shift from one role to another, for example, exercise or dressing. One telecommuter even installed an external door into his office to distinguish work from home (Evans, 1993).

Working at home blurs roles for the telecommuters's family as well. Children, spouses, neighbors, and even pets may find it difficult to know when the telecommuter is available for family-related interaction versus when they are working.[7] One telecommuter discusses the "general problem of dividing 'work' from 'home' life. How do you explain to a 2-year-old that daddy in the kitchen making a cup of coffee is thinking about his next paragraph and is not to be interrupted?" (Forester, 1988/1989, p. 218). Teleworkers adopt different patterns of negotiating work and home life—for some, work is prioritized over children and housework; for others (predominantly women), telework involves fitting in paid work around domestic responsibilities and patterns (Haddon & Silverstone, 1995).

IMPACT OF TELEWORK ON THE INDIVIDUAL AND FAMILY

Toffler's (1980) book, *The Third Wave*, predicted that technological innovations would engender "[a] return to cottage industry on a new, higher, electronic basis, and with it a new emphasis on the home as the center of society" (p. 210). This "new emphasis" is predicated on a return to the era of preindustrial cottage industries in which families labored together in the home or on the farm and is predicted by Toffler to incorporate greater involvement in the community, benefits to the environment, and healthier, deeper relationships. This Utopian interpretation of working at home ignores telework's more pragmatic concerns and focuses instead on the symbolism of returning to an era in which the home, not the workplace, served as society's focal point (Jackson & van der Wielen, 1998). More grounded work that investigates the effects of telework on family life has been inconclusive: while most mobile workers in one survey-based study reported that "mobility had positively influenced their ability to balance work and family life," a majority said they had either a "very difficult" or a "difficult" time balancing work and home life (Hill et al., 1996). However, another study suggests that working from home can assist parents in negotiating work and family demands (Duxbury, Higgins, & Neufeld, 1998).

These contradictory sentiments are not unusual. For many, the constant access to work provided by telecommuting can be mentally and physically unhealthy. Telework has the potential to exacerbate tendencies of "workaholism" (Olson, 1988b; Olson & Primps, 1990; Pratt, 1984), due to the easy and unfettered access to work and the lack of external cues that serve to signal when to stop working. In 1988, Olson noted that the availability of the computer makes it "tempting (particularly with electronic mail) to just sign on and 'check my mail' or 'see who else is on the system'" (1988b, p. 94). Given current rates of Internet use within the home, it is likely this tendency continues to be an issue for today's teleworkers. As one human resources researcher quipped, "Giving a workaholic a [portable computer] is like giving an alcoholic a bottle of gin" (Kaplan, 1996). For employees who use ICTs to work longer hours at home but do not receive any additional benefits, mobile work could in fact be detrimental to family and home life.

As a culture, we express feelings of anxiety about the amount of time we have at our disposal, although it is unclear whether we are working more than we were in earlier eras or less (Robinson & Godbey, 1997; Schor, 1991). A 1997 *Wall Street Journal* article on the topic summed up the "profound sense of time pressure Americans report in surveys" with its title: "Do We Work More or Not? Either Way, We Feel Frazzled" (Shellenbarger, 1997a, p. B1). Cultural anxieties about the rise of dual-income families have focused primarily on temporal pressures and the home: if both parents work, who will care for the children, clean the house, cook the meals?[8] There is some indication that work-at-home arrangements might ameliorate these concerns, assuming that teleworkers can integrate domestic chores into their paid work. For example, one homeworker told an interviewer, "I don't really mind homework . . . because when I'm home, I can have the laundry going when I am doing my homework" (Costello, 1988, p. 138). While some domestic chores (e.g., laundry) can be integrated with paid work fairly easily, research indicates that female teleworkers retain primary responsibility for household chores, which often leads to feelings of frustration, stress, and failure (Christensen, 1987/1988a, 1988b; Costello, 1988). This is particularly ironic given that telecommuting is often portrayed as a means by which women may successfully balance work and family life (Mirchandani, 1998b). It is true that some female telecommuters claim working at home is the best of both worlds (Dickerson, 1998a). However, evidence suggests that traditional gender roles regarding child care and domestic duties are often unaffected by the professional status of women, especially if they are working at home. So, even though dual-wage families are becoming more prevalent, women retain responsibility for the majority of the (unpaid) household work in addition to their paid work outside the home (Christensen, 1988b; Costello, 1988; Mirchandani, 1998a).[9]

Although telework is often conceived of as a way to care for children while completing paid work (Mirchandani, 1998b), there is little evidence that it is possible to simultaneously do both (Ahrentzen, 1990; Christensen, 1987/ 1988a). Critics contend that this vision of telecommuting assumes that neither work responsibilities nor family responsibilities are important enough to warrant full-time attention, and they critique telecommuting as encouraging the "transmutation of societal obligations into women's obligations, while simultaneously serving the ends of the pro-family movement, which seeks to re-create the nuclear family" (Zimmerman, 1986/1990, p. 202). Not surprisingly, male teleworkers who typically did not simultaneously work and care for children reported *decreased* stress levels, whereas women teleworkers with child care responsibilities reported *increased* levels of stress working at home (Olson & Primps, 1990). Costello (1988) discusses the case of one husband who initially encouraged his wife to telecommute but later told her "I don't care, the money is not worth it. I can't stay down in the family room [with the children] one more night" (p. 140). Regardless, working at home as a strategy by which working parents might spend time with their children is receiving more attention, especially from women. These so-called mamapreneurs have inspired a bevy of books, magazines, and Web sites (Dickerson, 1998b). In fact, a survey of Southern California women-owned businesses found that nearly one in three were home based (Dickerson, 1998a).

Others critique telecommuting as a means by which capitalist interests might further disempower individual workers, especially women:

The much-acclaimed computerized retreat to the electronic cottage thus appears less a vision of "progress" than a backward glance through a rearview mirror. Rather than a stop en route to an even better artisan age, the electronic cottage heralds another form of owner-controlled, supervised, and rationalized labor. (Zimmerman, 1986/1990, p. 205)

It is true that teleworkers are more vulnerable to exploitation, given the difficulty of monitoring private homes and the unresolved legal issues surrounding telework. For instance, the extent to which teleworkers are protected legally while working at home is unclear. Legally, telework disrupts certain established boundaries: organizations must attempt to certify that teleworkers have safe and adequate work space in their homes, yet in doing so expose themselves to invasion of privacy litigation (Armour, 1998). Also, many fear that firms will use telework as a way to transform full-time jobs with benefits into contract positions, which typically have no benefits (Christensen, 1987/1988a). Unions and labor activists have expressed the concern that telework will have a detrimental effect on worker solidarity because there is no collective workplace in which to organize (Holderness, 1995; Kraut, 1987; Pratt, 1984).

The following two chapters will discuss the case studies of iLAN Systems and XYZ, focusing specifically on issues of management, home/work boundaries, transfer of organizational knowledge, and interpersonal communication among distributed workers.

Chapter Three

iLAN Systems: A Distributed Work Environment from Inception

iLAN Systems is in many ways an exemplar of the virtual organization described by Nohria and Berkley (1994) as the "organization of the future": its structure reshaped by technology and a new emphasis on knowledge as capital. The company sells no tangible products, although some of the training materials do arrive in packages. Rather, iLAN sells the labor and expertise of its technicians, who work primarily on computer networks.

iLAN has been virtual from inception. All employees were hired with the explicit understanding that the corporate perks would not include a secretary and a cubicle—rather, technicians would spend most of their time at client sites. The company has no corporate headquarters; the "suite" listed on business cards is actually a mailbox at a Mail Boxes Etc. franchise. The ways in which iLAN's culture both supported and was challenged by telework is the focus of this chapter.

ORGANIZATIONAL HISTORY AND STRUCTURE

iLAN Systems was started when cofounder Tom Reynolds left his sales position at a large technology company where he had worked for almost a decade.[1] He and another employee, Dave Lee, had discussed starting a company six months prior to Reynolds's departure, and in 1993, the two started iLAN. According to *Cyberlane Commuter*, the book coauthored by Reynolds and an iLAN employee, the company generated revenues of over $6 million in both 1996 and 1997 (Reynolds & Brusseau, 1998, p. 27).

As a general rule, iLAN's employee base fluctuates from 40 to 70 employees, but many of these employees are contracted out to other companies.[2] These employees, who are out-sourced for months at a time, were not considered in this study because in many ways they do not function, nor do they identify themselves, as iLAN employees. iLAN's core set of employees typically consists of support personnel (four sales and marketing/recruiting personnel and two administrative/ accountant personnel) and operations personnel (seven or so network engineers). The two owners, Tom Reynolds and Dave Lee, also do some of this "delivery" work. The company's net-work engineers are the epitome of the mobile worker: they enjoy sophisticated communications technology and typically work either from home, from the Help Desk, or from customer sites. Most of the employees have a workspace at home, al-though the technicians who do the network delivery work spend a good part of their time at customer sites. For a fee, iLAN also offers technical consulting that can be conducted over the phone or through software that allows technicians to view and control the desktop of a user's computer.

Although originally a purely virtual company without any leased office space, in mid-1997 the company rented office space in an area close to the founders' homes. Employees use this area to assemble hardware, hold monthly meetings, and answer customer support calls. This Help Desk was created at the request of a large client that wanted a place to test server equipment and was retained by iLAN after that contract was completed. The building is a 1,500 square foot industrial office space that contains two small offices, a larger room with com-puters in various stages of assembly, and the Help Desk itself, essentially a room encircled by a long counter holding phones, computers, software manuals, and other troubleshooting ne-cessities. It is usually staffed by at least one person during tra-ditional working hours, although the phone lines can also be forwarded to employees' houses.

Technicians are not required to check into the Help Desk every morning: sometimes they will go straight to a client's site from their homes, other times they will meet at the Help Desk and then dis-perse. Typically, technicians appear at the Help Desk sporadically throughout the day, for various reasons and as schedules permit, but as a rule do not spend entire days there. This behavior is clearly encouraged by one of the founders, Dave Lee. At his previous job,

Lee was rarely in the office. As he describes it, his coworkers assumed he was not working because he was not visible on a daily basis. However, when significant layoffs occurred, he was one of the few people not to lose his job. While his colleagues maintained a stronger presence at the office, he was more productive. In contrast to research on telecommuters that points to the connection some perceive between employee visibility and career development, Lee's absence in the office meant that he was spending more time with clients and therefore generating more sales. Lee clearly associates productivity with being out in the field, and this attitude permeates iLAN's organizational culture.

The Help Desk provides a physical space that enables employees to communicate organizational knowledge and technical information to one another through face-to-face, informal communication. One support employee who did not have a technical background went to the Help Desk specifically to enhance his technical knowledge. At the Help Desk, he could "hang out with [the technicians] and just kind of listen to them talk. And interact with them a little bit because then I can pick up a few more things to learn. . . . Pick their brains." These types of spontaneous interactions did not tap company or personal resources in the way a phone call might, because questions could be timed to fill the spaces in between client calls.

In addition to its core support and operations employees, the company employs a number of technicians who are outsourced and, therefore, although technically iLAN employees, do not report to the Help Desk and interact only marginally with the core iLAN employees. iLAN outsources network specialists and other highly specialized technical personnel to companies as part of their "employment services." At one time, iLAN had as many as 46 employees working for a major Southern California aerospace company, which was very lucrative for the company, although in response to economic pressures, this number decreased substantially.[3] These outsourced technicians, hired by iLAN, typically report to other sites for months at a time, although iLAN handles their salaries and administrative details, such as benefits and health insurance claims. According to Reynolds, employees who work for their major client, a large engineering firm, are less productive and have higher turnover rates than employees who work directly for iLAN. He attributes this to the difference in the firms' culture. Employees who had experienced both environments agreed with this assessment. Describing this other company as "corporate, hierarchical, authority driven," one iLAN employee laughingly pointed to his bare feet during a home interview to illustrate the differences in culture between the two companies. Several iLAN employees worked at one of these companies before they came to iLAN, and claim to enjoy working at iLAN more.

iLAN offers network support services, primarily trouble-shooting, but also conducts network assessment, design, in-stallation, and support. This type of work requires the company to be extremely responsive, particularly to emer-gency calls. The emergency phone number is staffed 24 hours a day: at night and on weekends, it rings in the home of one of the engineers. Reynolds feels that emergencies are what iLAN does best, and the fact that iLAN identifies itself as an expert in this type of emergency-response work has a large impact on the structure and the culture of the firm.

Emergency response is an area that generates new business for the company and can be quite lucrative. For most organiza-tions that rely on communication technology, a network that is not functioning can bring the entire business to a halt. Malfunc-tioning networks mean that employees cannot access e-mail and Intranets; a Web site that is not accepting visitors can mean loss of revenue, credibility, and clients. By the time they contact iLAN, organizations suffering from a downed network are usually quite agitated. As one iLAN employee explains, "They wanted us there yesterday."

This aspect of the business also affects the hours worked by employees, some of whom will work longer than the traditional 40-hour workweek to respond to emergencies or complete work that cannot be done during working hours, such as server in-stallations. After working a night shift, iLAN employees can sometimes arrange to take time off during the normal workweek, although this is an informal arrangement rather than a carefully tabulated reimbursement. In fact, iLAN claims that their em-ployees work an average of two extra hours a day over employees of traditional organizations, some of which is time recouped from saved travel (Reynolds & Brusseau, 1998, p. 31).

iLAN has attempted to capture a niche market consisting of telecommuters who may not have access to technical support by repackaging the Help Desk as a resource for telecommuters. Reynolds feels the issue of technical support for telecommuters is an often overlooked albeit critical element in determining the success of a telecommuting project and that the lack of support for telecommuters may account for productivity losses.[4] He points out that telecommuters are typically unable to access in-house technical resources and must instead act as their own technical support, a time-consuming chore.

The company is clearly attempting to position itself as an expert in telecommuting issues and a leader in the telecommuting support arena. To this end, iLAN president Tom Reynolds and an iLAN employee coauthored their book on the subject *Cyberlane Commuter. Cybercommuting* is the term they coined to refer to "the marriage of telecommuting and the World Wide Web" (Reynolds & Brusseau, 1998, p. 150). As their promotional material and their book explain, "The cybercommuter lives and works on the Web, using and sharing cyberdata, communicating with cyberprocesses, and collaborating with cybercolleagues with cybertools" (p. 150). The *cyberlane* is defined as "the office environment created in the home. Quality access to the Internet and the corporate network and professional support of the home environment" (p. 151).

The company is extremely savvy about exploiting any mention of the company for promotional purposes. For instance, a full-color reproduction of an article in the *Los Angeles Times* that mentions the company is included in their promotional materials and is referenced several times in *Cyberlane Commuter.* In the original, a picture of Reynolds in his home office is included on the second page. In the version included in iLAN's promotional materials, the layout of the article has been instrumentally altered so that the picture of Reynolds is on the front page. The other photos from the original piece are not reproduced.

AN ANTIBUREAUCRATIC PHILOSOPHY

From its inception, iLAN Systems was designed to be a distributed company. Reynolds and Brusseau's book, which excoriates another organization's "meeting culture," details the hours wasted in meetings "where we sat in a big conference room around an oval table and planned . . . talked about planning . . . and planned to meet again to plan some more" (1998, p. 12). Reynolds writes that when he created iLAN:

> I was determined to create a culture of productivity not bogged down by needless bureaucratic or feel-good processes. I concluded that the only way this could happen was to NOT have a central office—NOT one square foot of office space. Except for our very crowded break/fix lab where a few technicians run our Help Desk, there is literally no place for people to get together and have a meeting. Our corporate address . . . is a

post office box. I did this on purpose to set a cultural tone for the company. (p. 27)

Reynolds claims iLAN's low turnover rate is due to its employees' ability to telecommute, and the employees who telework claim to be more productive and to prefer it to traditional work arrangements. Sometimes the ability to telecommute has allowed employees to make positive changes in their lives. For instance, one employee was able to move into his elderly mother's home and was therefore available for trips to the doctor's office and the grocery store. In another case, an employee who was recovering from chemotherapy was able to work from home and avoid a draining commute.

An extremely influential aspect of iLAN's culture revolves around its status as a "virtual company" (Reynolds & Brusseau, 1998, p. 52), and therefore, more enlightened than traditional space- and time-bound companies. One oft-repeated story has assumed almost mythic status among iLAN employees:

> The regional sales manager for [a large technology company] . . . was paying us a sales visit one day, and telephoned us, somewhat bewildered, from a phone booth asking where we were. He had never visited us before and was standing outside the Mail Boxes Etc. store we use as the address on our cards and letterhead. We directed him to our Help Desk and he arrived very relieved to know that we really did exist, although not in the traditional form that he was used to visiting! (Reynolds & Brusseau, 1998, p. 52)

This tale functions in two ways within the iLAN culture. It both emphasizes iLAN's status as virtual while calling attention to the constricted, limiting nature of traditional thinking. While illustrating iLAN's disregard for geographical trappings, it also emphasizes the traditional business world's stodgy reliance on them. Retelling this story serves to solidify iLAN's progressive self-image: the visiting manager is presented as intellectually narrow and outdated, but more importantly, so is the organizational paradigm he represents. This dichotomy is highlighted in a company engineer's retelling of the story:

> Tom has told the story about one guy who called who went to our mailing address. And so he's standing outside of Mail Boxes Etc., going "Well, where are you?" and the answer is, "Not there!" . . . Some clients, it doesn't bother; some, it's

like, "Oh, you mean you don't have *real* offices." . . . There is
that sort of cultural mind-set. With some people it's like,
"Oh, that's wonderful." Others . . . they were expecting an
office: if you have a company, you have an office.

iLAN's lack of a central office is made possible by its
incorporation of ICTs into almost every aspect of the work
process. iLAN employees use technological tools to process
and receive information and to communicate with their
clients and coworkers. For the most part, they seemed gen-
uinely enthusiastic about technology—even the Human Resources person, who did not play a technical role within the
organization, spent 15 minutes proudly fiddling with his
videoconferencing technology during an interview. This fond-
ness for technology, however, made the computers in their
homes a seductive distraction. Access to the Internet at any
hour of the day or night often resulted in employees going
into their home offices to write down a thought or quickly
check e-mail and getting immersed in a task. Employees' proclivity for losing track of time sometimes caused tensions with
family members, who perceived them as being less available
for family interaction and shirking household duties.

As a rule, iLAN employees are given the technical tools they
need to do their jobs. The one time an employee did not have a necessary piece of equipment—in this case, a printer—he admitted
that it was his fault and that the company would reimburse him if
and when he made the purchase. Depending on the type of work
done, iLAN employees are typically provided with pagers, fast connections to the Internet (ISDN or frame relay), cellular phones, and,
for some of the technicians, portable Nextel phones with walkie-
talkie features. Through a policy of quickly returning calls, its heavy
investment in technology equipment, and a robust network, iLAN
seems to have avoided some of the communication problems often
associated with distributed work.

This emphasis on rapid communication and immediate
availability is critical for a company that is both incident driven
and highly technical. Continual employee availability is also
important for the company's troubleshooting efforts. No one
employee can be expected to be fluent in all of the software pro-
grams iLAN supports, but with reliable communication and an
updated database linking individuals and their areas of expertise, a technician's ability to solve a customer's problem is
greatly increased. This intelligent use of networking technology
allows iLAN to exploit the knowledge base of its distributed

workforce, as opposed to some distributed work environments in which the organization's ability to tap into its employee knowledge base is compromised.

Organizational Culture

iLAN's culture and structure is heavily influenced by the company's focus on network troubleshooting, which is highly technical work coupled with an inflexible temporal structure. Within the organization, emphasis is placed on accountability and responsiveness, codified in the company standard that states employees must respond to pages or calls within 15 minutes during regular working hours and within 1 hour on weekends.

"Fighting Fires" and "Hunting Bears"

One support employee explained the need for iLAN's responsiveness with the following analogy: "When a customer's computer is down, it's like their house is burning, okay? Their house is on fire and they need someone to put it out. And if you can't respond quickly to the customer, you're out of there." A company engineer echoed this characterization of iLAN employees as rescue workers, gripping computer cables instead of water: "We're like the firefighters." In fact, the metaphors used to describe the organization by its members are very action and response oriented, with overtones of cowboy machismo.

The metaphor of the hunt also figures prominently within iLAN's organizational culture. Within the scenario of this metaphor, the client is typically represented as the prey to be captured while the sales and marketing people are hunting dogs, poised to flush the prey out of the bushes, or are "door kickers" who "kick down the door" to get one of the founders inside to complete the deal. One support employee who works in a recruiting capacity, primarily attempting to generate new business, explains his role as that of a bird dog: "Since I'm not a technical person, we've been team selling. I'm the bird dog. I get the hunter to the door—Tom Reynolds—and hopefully it'll flush and we'll get a shot."

In another telling use of a hunting metaphor, a marketing person was said to be out "getting bears," in reference to a joke popular with the engineers. In the joke, a salesperson and an engineer go hunting. They get to the cabin where they will be staying and the salesperson goes out straightaway to start hunting, while the engineer stays behind to get the cabin cleaned up and suitable for habitation. After a while, he hears some shouts: "Open the door! I've got a bear!" He opens the door and the "marketeer" runs in, followed closely by a grizzly bear. The salesperson runs through the cabin and out an open window, leaving the engineer in the cabin with the huge, angry bear. And as the marketeer is diving out the back window he says, "I got the bear in the cabin—it's up to you to skin him!" (iLAN engineer).

This story aptly encapsulates the sometimes antagonistic, paradoxical relationship between the sales and engineering divisions in many organizations, as Kunda (1992) has noted and Scott Adams has exploited in his "Dilbert" comic strip (Aden, 1998). The tension inherent in the relationship stems from the fact that the salesperson and the engineer have vastly different skill sets, training, and motivations, yet are symbiotically dependent on each other. The salesperson is reliant on and excels in interfacing with people, whereas many engineers interface primarily with technology. The tension stems from the fact that while the salesperson creates work (job security, compensation, and the ability to do what one loves for a living) for the engineer, he or she can simultaneously make life miserable for the engineer by agreeing to difficult deadlines or impossible feature sets. Whether this is done out of benevolent technical ineptitude, a well-intentioned desire to close a deal, or malice depends on the interpretation of the engineer. Although the inspiration for jokes, relationships between sales and engineering types at iLAN do not seem to be a source of antipathy. This may stem from the fact that the salespeople are discouraged from discussing technical specifics with the client, leaving this work instead to those with more technical expertise.

INFLUENCE OF THE FOUNDERS

iLAN is a classic example of a small firm in which the culture is influenced dramatically by the founders. There are no earnest discussions about democracy in the workplace; rather, the founders make decisions about how the organization is run and who does what. Paradoxically, the organization also functions as an extremely open system. Employees are encouraged to articulate suggestions, although the founders make the final decision about whether a specific idea will be implemented.

The assumptions and beliefs of the founder of an organization, although they may be modified with the passage of time, will have a large impact on an organization's culture (Schein, 1985). iLAN is an example of a firm greatly influenced both structurally and culturally by its two founders. For instance, Reynolds characterizes himself and Lee as "rough-and-tumble kinds of guys": "This company is rough and tumble because of both Dave and I. I want to use the words *rough and tumble* meaning . . . we express ourselves without regard to how it's going to affect people's feelings. . . . The test is 'is this the truth?' not 'will this hurt your feelings?'"

Reynolds's distaste for bureaucracy can be seen in the lack of a static organizational chart that lists specific details about titles, supervisory roles, or job duties. Rather, these are handled on a case-by-case basis. In the lingo of the trade, the organizational chart is "rendered on the fly" rather than existing as a static document to be accessed by many but altered by only a few. More than one employee, when queried about their job responsibilities, indicated that their duties were defined by the owners' wishes. In essence, their responsibilities could be distilled to doing whatever needed to be done to keep the owners happy: "Whatever Tom and Dave want," one iLAN engineer stated.

Many employees remarked on the different roles of the two owners within the organization and the functions they performed. Dave Lee, described by one employee as the "network and problem-solver guy," handles the technical aspects of the company's network troubleshooting business. He often does the initial high-level planning and network mapping work, leaving the lower level implementation work to technicians that follow his lead, and is described as more detail oriented than Reynolds. Lee also serves as the chief financial officer for the company and, within this role, keeps an eye on the company's expenditures and its income from billable work.

Reynolds, on the other hand, is the "vision guy" of the company, the one who comes up with ideas but typically allows others to worry about specific implementation details. One support employee described the differences between the founders by explaining: "Lee's focus is very technically oriented and runs the operation technically for the company. Reynolds is more a visionary and it's better for all of us when he kind of stays away and sits there up at his house and just thinks, because that's really important for the company."

A company engineer explained the difference between the two founders in similar terms: "Reynolds is more [of a] 100,000-foot-level person," whereas "Lee is down at the 2-inch level. He wants everything in dollars and cents and [is concerned with] . . . profit, so there's a different view of the world if you will. Lee typically wants more detail backup than Reynolds does."

The influence of the founders and their "rough-and-tumble" emphasis on efficiency over social niceties can also be seen in the company's aversion to meetings. The company has one meeting a month, which all employees, except for two administrative staff people, attend. According to *Cyberlane Commuter*, these meetings last 1 hour and "everyone attending that meeting holds our feet to the fire if we get off onto tangents" (p. 91). Reynolds's distaste for meetings is documented throughout *Cyberlane Commuter* in anecdotes and truisms. His "Rule #28," for instance, is "Meetings promote meetings, not consensus" (p. 15).

In the book, meetings are presented as an occasion for posturing, inefficiency, and indecisiveness. However, another function of meetings is that they allow members to trade information about styles of negotiation, communication, and idiosyncrasies, which might improve productivity over the long run (Weick, 1979). However, given that iLAN's meetings do not need to result in consensus, this is not necessarily a benefit for iLAN.

"ROUGH-AND-TUMBLE" TROUBLESHOOTING

The promotional brochure for iLAN's network troubleshooting business exemplifies the organization's cultural emphasis on fast response time, technical expertise, and cowboy machismo. Cowboy-cum-technician Dave Lee, dressed in leather chaps, a western-style shirt, and cowboy hat, graces the cover. He holds a cellular phone to his ear and stands next to a large traveling case suitable for transporting a laptop computer and other technical gear. The handle of a shiny gun sticks out of the holster on his hip. The brochure's text praises iLAN's technical support and develops the analogy that other companies are essentially blindfolded in the fight against network trouble because they are not trained as well as iLAN technicians: "Network trouble-shooting is a lot like a gunfight. Anyone can participate but only the experts survive." The brochure depicts a blindfolded gunfighter (presumably the "other guys") haphazardly shooting holes in nearby cacti, barrels, and buckets. Meanwhile, a confident Dave Lee smiles at the camera, looking very much like a man who just blew the smoke from his barrel after a successful network troubleshooting episode.

This Wild West imagery is carried throughout the brochure. The attached business card is labeled with the cautionary note: "Save this card . . . you'll need it!" and promises that "When you need help fast, iLAN's [technicians] are only a phone call away— they'll keep your network street fight from turning into the OK Corral!" The business card includes a picture of a silver handgun screened behind the contact information for Dave "Wyatt" Lee and reads "HAVE SNIFFER WILL TRAVEL."[5]

The company perceives (and is clearly attempting to present) the world of computer networks as a sort of battle or gunfight in which iLAN has the tools, the expertise, and the attitude to win. The photograph on the cover, in which Dave Lee has all the accoutrements of the modern-day cowboy, exemplifies this melding of Wild West and cutting-edge technology. Instead of holding a gun, he holds a mobile phone firmly to his ear. This image clearly represents iLAN's belief that the critical weapons of the modern-age standoff are not bullets but responsiveness and access to accurate, timely information—both enabled by ICTs.

Lee's discussion of the way in which the Web site has replaced the traditional office is also illustrative of this paradigm shift from the tangible to the intangible:

> At the beginning when we started, there was [the idea that if] you don't have an office . . . you are a fly-by-night company. And that was at the beginning. Nowadays, they think that's the greatest thing since sliced bread. Because now it's the trend. We were ahead of our time. At that time they thought we were fly-by-night. Matter of fact, some of the companies tried to come over and visit us and ended up at the Mail Boxes Etc. place. "What kind of fly-by-night outfit are you?" Now, [if] you don't have a Web site, you're not a real company. . . . That's because of the advent of the Internet. Everybody has access to it now; everybody who needs information will go to the Internet and look it up. It's become the most important piece of information now—as opposed to your office. They don't care about your office now, with all the flags flying in front of it.

According to Lee, the emphasis on traditional indicators of prosperity and legitimacy, a company's office space and appearance, has shifted. To be perceived as a legitimate company in this economy one must have a well-designed Web site and an easy-to-remember domain name. This shift mirrors the shift

Bell (1973) and others have discussed, from goods to information. As Lee argues, the information presented on a company's Web site and the style with which it is presented is more important than the appearance and zip code of its office building. The bricks and mortar that previously signified an organization's legitimacy have been replaced by the bits and bytes that represent its intellectual capital. Although skeptics might argue that a sophisticated Web site can create false assumptions about the legitimacy of an organization, it should be noted that office space, employees, and furniture can easily be rented to create the same illusion.

HIERARCHY AND DIVISION OF LABOR

At iLAN Systems, employees are extremely flexible about their job responsibilities and seem more swayed by leadership and necessity than by hierarchy or highly codified position descriptions. For instance, one employee, when asked about his job title, had to confirm it by consulting his business card. Others appeared to invent titles on the spot or frankly stated that the title didn't "mean a thing." Job responsibilities were similarly flexible; one employee, when asked about his job responsibilities, said, "Whatever Tom and Dave want me to do." This sort of flexibility echoes Nohria and Berkley's (1994) delineation of the virtual organization, where we see the "implosion of bureaucratic specialization into 'global,' cross-functional, computer-mediated jobs, such that individual members . . . may be considered holographically equivalent to the organization as a whole" (p. 115). One iLAN support employee, speaking to this widened conception of task and responsibility, explained:

> The bottom line is that Tom and Dave are the owners and everyone needs to make sure that [their] wishes are followed. So you know what you need to do. If you are doing one thing and you know there's something else that's important to the owners, you don't have a supervisor making that decision for you. You know that you have to do it. So do I report to [my immediate supervisor]? Yes, technically, but [he] doesn't ever call me and ask me what I'm doing, ever, ever ever ever. Not ever.

At iLAN, there seems to be little compartmentalization of responsibility. While this may be due in part to the fact that it is a smaller company with little administrative support, employees are responsive to internal needs that arise, regardless of their official duties. As the support employee quoted above went on to explain:

> Certainly if [my supervisor] called me up and asked me to do something, I certainly would. But than again if somebody over at the lab who's lateral or even below me called me up and said "Could you help me with this project?" I would help. So what we do in the company, probably because of the nature of the organization being spread out, and everyone [working] from their house, the bottom line is you do what's good for the company. And if it's a good move for the company then it's in your best interest to do it.

Clearly, iLAN employees identify with the company and its success is important to them. A married couple that both work for iLAN from their home demonstrated this global sense of duty that is not limited to individual duties but rather "what is good for the company":

> PETE: Linda gets the calls. But you saw me pick up the phone. That's another example—
>
> LINDA: If it's closer to him he'll answer it. If it's over here I'll answer it.
>
> PETE: That's a good example of how the company works. If you're in a suit mentality, in a corporate regimented, hierarchical environment, I would not answer the phone—
>
> LINDA: He'd be yelling, "Linda, your phone is ringing!"

Other employees made similar comparisons between iLAN's culture and traditional "regimented" organizations that assume, as one engineer said, "if you have a company you have an office." No employees gave any indication that they preferred a traditional organizational structure.

FUNCTIONAL FRAGMENTATION AND MONITORING

Employees of iLAN Systems typically serve one of two functions: either technical (network engineers) or support, which is nontechnical (e.g., human resources, recruitment, accounts payable). While the latter group uses computers to get their work done, they do not typically repair them, analyze them, or "look under the hood" so to speak. This division of labor also impacts the communicative structure of the organization. In the words of one nontechnical employee, the engineers were "talking a different language." A nontechnical employee explained that "when [a technician] talks to [a nontechnical employee] about a server, [the technician] is saying, 'the code layer of the application is . . .' and [the nontechnical employee] hears [gibberish]." Another support employee freely admitted that she was unable to understand what the engineers were talking about at a recent company meeting. This lack of a shared language was probably exacerbated by the fact that operational and support personnel interacted with each other only sporadically.

As discussed in the previous chapter, much of the literature on telecommuting stresses that supervision is one of the primary areas of concern, especially for managers. The overarching challenge becomes one of supervising (from the Latin *vidēre*, to see) those you cannot see. At iLAN, the combination of a dispersed work environment and a work population fragmented into technical and nontechnical paradigms created a situation in which management from afar proved particularly challenging. Because both of the founders came from a technical background, they did not have a deep understanding of the nature of the work done by some of the support personnel, especially those involved in human resources or marketing. This inevitably led to some anxiety about the support employees' daily activities and accomplishments on the part of the founders. During a discussion among the two support employees and their immediate supervisor at the time, the supervisor explained, "When Dave is not up to his neck in delivery work, he tends to try and focus on the dollar picture of the company and part of that is, what are those guys over in [the beach community where the two support employees live] doing for me?" One of the employees in question agreed, "Exactly. Are they down at the beach?" To this, the supervisor described the thought process of the founder in more detail: "Are they at the beach *at the beach* or at the beach *working*? How am I going to tell that?"

The lack of geographical proximity combined with the functional difference between support jobs and engineering enhanced underlying tensions surrounding the supervision of these off-site employees. In an attempt to manage these tensions, the company built a software database called "Net-Nag" that tracked the accountability of these two support personnel. As one of NetNag's creators explained:

> Their work isn't as measurable. Like technicians, Lee sends
> a technician out to fix a network problem at some cus-
> tomer's office. He comes back and Lee says, "How'd it go?"
> "Well, we had to move this router and I had to remap it and
> here's the map." So he gets that feedback. Support person-
> nel, it's harder. And that's hard in any environment, but in
> a telecommuting environment, it's harder . . . he's not get-
> ting this feedback. And I saw that, so I thought it's probably
> important to have some kind of hard reporting so that be-
> comes kind of the window on [the employees], versus walk-
> ing past their cubicle and glancing in and seeing crap all
> over the floor and [one employee] stuffing envelopes and
> [the other] dialing for dollars.

As illustrated by this quote, the fragmentation between the technical
and nontechnical employees is further exacerbated by the spatial
dispersion of the organization. The two employees in question lived
about an hour's drive from the Help Desk, which disinclined them to
stop by the Help Desk. A company employee, who worked closely
with these employees, described the phenomenon in these terms:

> Linda is knee-deep in the [human resources] thing. She's
> the only person in the company, almost, that does that! So
> there's a whole raft of functionality that no one else in the
> company can relate to because they don't deal with it! And
> she is 43 miles away from everybody else. So there's very lit-
> tle transfer of information, if you will, about HR activities to
> the rest of the world. . . . It's not like in an office environ-
> ment where you have functionality sprinkled over . . . inter-
> mixed in an office environment. Even if you start out on day
> one where you've got HR over here on the left, engineering
> over on the right, marketing in the middle, over time offices
> tend to . . . kind of mush together. As a due matter of
> course, you walk into the elevator, you say hello to your
> neighbor. He's in a different functionality than you are, so
> you pick up kind of a flavor of the activities he's involved in
> or the kind of problems he is having. You don't get that at
> iLAN, because there isn't this watercooler effect. There's
> some amount of "what the heck is going on over there!"

Because iLAN's founders are technicians, it is easier for them
to monitor and understand the products of the engineers on staff.
In a reversal from the more common situation in which management finds it more difficult to monitor technicians because they

typically do not produce tangible results, in this case, as one support employee explained, "It's hard for [the founders] to see because [the support people] aren't technical. They aren't going out and solving network problems." These employees typically performed tasks that had fewer immediate and objectively measurable results and were not billable. Understandably, the founders were less able to answer the question, "What the heck is going on over there?"

iLAN's solution was for these employees to produce additional documentation legitimizing their contribution to the organization. Initially, the documentation was a weekly report detailing that week's work products. Later, for one of the support employees, this became a daily report, listing metrics agreed to by both the employee and his supervisor. The indirect manager and the employee assessed the job requirements and determined appropriate metrics based on specific tasks that could be measured empirically each day: the number of phone calls, the number of promotional packets sent out, and the number of bookings. The results of each day's labor were e-mailed to the supervisor. For unrelated reasons, both employees left the firm within a few months of the implementation of this scheme. However, it is worth noting that this scheme emphasized tasks that could be empirically measured, and de-legitimized work that produced intangible (though perhaps invaluable) results.

Because of the ways in which iLAN was created, structured, and managed, the company faced different and in some ways less challenging obstacles than did the second organization studied, XYZ. The contrast between the two organizations will serve to highlight differences in the way telework was socially shaped by employees, managers, and family members. The next chapter will discuss XYZ's transition to a telework scheme and some of the changes that accompanied it.

Chapter Four

XYZ:
Remote Management's Commitment to Telework

The sales division of XYZ utilized telework and mobile work strategies with the goal of increasing productivity, cutting real estate costs, and making their salespeople more comfortable with the company's telecommuting products. Key differences between XYZ and iLAN Systems involve the way in which telework was introduced, the company's motivation for adopting it, the support it received from management, and the degree to which teleworkers were given the tools they needed to maximize productivity and minimize problems associated with working at home. XYZ experienced a high degree of organizational and structural change during the period of this study, and this affected the ways in which telework was both implemented by the organization and socially shaped by the individual.[1]

ORGANIZATIONAL HISTORY AND STRUCTURE

XYZ, a subsidiary of the U.S. branch of a large Japanese technology firm that produces a wide array of technology-based products and services, was created in 1988 through the merger of three organizations. During the data collection period, XYZ's Japanese parent company employed more than 160,000 people worldwide and claimed more than $30 billion in annual revenue. One of 16 subsidiaries of Comco in the United States alone, XYZ's focus was selling Comco's communications technology, such as private branch exchange products, which allow multiple users to share external phone lines. Clients were primarily large organizations, such as government offices or school districts. The XYZ business unit was closed in 2001 when the company restructured its business.

The decision to "mobilize" (XYZ's preferred term for its telework initiative) its sales staff was made by top management and was initially implemented in two branch offices in California, Culver City and Anaheim, which are the subject of this study. The sales staff at XYZ is a well-defined hierarchy in which account executives report to sales managers who in turn report to a general manager. General managers report to the regional manager for their geographic area (for instance, the U.S. Southwest). According to the organizational chart, this regional manager then reports to the president. For most of the duration of this study, however, all sales employees of the three Southern California offices (Anaheim, Culver City, and Irvine before it was closed) reported to the regional manager.

CULVER CITY OFFICE TELEWORK PROGRAM

In late 1996, XYZ management in the Culver City, California, office announced that the office's sales staff would become "mobile workers." According to the new plan, account executives would no longer occupy individual permanent offices. They would instead utilize ICTs such as cell phones, call distribution systems, and laptop computers to work from their homes, on the road, and from client sites. This shift, from a traditional office structure to a collapsible one that could follow the worker, was only one aspect of a process that would evolve into a much more fundamental reorganization in which three Southern California districts were consolidated into one larger sales region. This shift enabled a reduction in middle managers and salespeople and permitted XYZ to reorganize its sales units. In the new scheme, sales professionals would be assigned vertical markets, such as health care, as opposed to a specific geographic territory.

A number of reasons were cited for the initial shift to mobile work. It was thought that the familiarity gained through increased use of the company's technological tools would increase salespeople's enthusiasm for and knowledge of Comco's "telecommuting solution" products. Also, salespeople who focused on one particular market would "own" that market—they would gain area-specific subject knowledge, identify more deeply with their focus area, and network with higher level executives within their field or specialty (as opposed to only interfacing with telecommunications managers). Focusing on a particular industry would also encourage sales representatives to develop a deeper, more specialized knowledge of the few products specific to that particular industry, as opposed to being superficially acquainted with the dozens of products Comco planned to support by the end of that year. It was thought that by "segmenting" the salespeople, it would help them focus and (as one salesperson aptly summarized) "talk the talk." Other reasons cited for the move were financial savings on real estate, improved morale, increased time spent working, better access to information, and decreased turnover.

Another factor, which evolved from historical circumstances, was the fact that the Culver City office's lease had expired, creating the opportunity to relocate to a smaller, more stylish office. The former office was in a modest, one-story, warehouse-style office building in an industrial area. Because the space was larger than the company needed, conference rooms and desks often were empty or underutilized.

In January 1997, XYZ relocated to a more upscale and sophisticated building about a half mile away. This new office building looked more like a high-level executive facility, with a sculptured fountain outside the spacious lobby, which boasted a fresh-flower display and two security guards. These new offices were 10,000 square feet smaller than the old building and cost less to lease. Since there were not enough desks in the new office to support a one-to-one desk-to-person ratio, a combination hoteling/telecommuting scheme was implemented. An area in the new building was outfitted with six desks, phones, and data ports, to be shared by the sales staff and other employees who worked in the office on a temporary basis.

As it turned out, though, layoffs occurred soon after the move. This was a tense and tumultuous period in which employees were removed from their permanent offices, were not given adequate technological support, and witnessed their colleagues' departures. There was a loss of morale and direction associated with both the movement to telework and the layoffs. This period of transition was difficult for many employees, who had to adjust to a new working environment as well as the uncertainty that accompanies this type of organizational change.

The layoffs reduced the number of staff so that it was possible for each employee to have his or her own dedicated cubicle. However, other associates of the company frequently worked in the Culver City office on a temporary basis. This was not a problem at the old location, which had 18 cubicles, but there was the potential for space to become an issue at the new, smaller office. After a period of experimentation with the vertical market approach, the sales staff returned to an open territory approach in which account executives were free to initiate contact with any potential customer.

At XYZ, account executives focus on making sales; they prospect for leads, try to close sales, and are the primary interface to clients and customers. They rely on sales engineers to provide technical support and to design and price systems based on customer requirements. An account executive and a sales engineer will often go on sales calls together and will work together to process bid requests from potential customers.

Although the Culver City employees generally expressed enthusiasm for the virtual office project, the transition to telecommuting seemed fraught with uncertainty. At one point a manager jokingly referred to the process as a model of "how *not* to do it." Initially, a lack of clarity about the shift to telework also made it difficult for employees to understand why it was done and what was expected of them. For instance, during one interview a salesperson explained that sometimes she wanted to "*go somewhere*" instead of working from home all the time. Her supervisor gently corrected her, saying "We don't want you *not* coming into the office . . . we want a *collapsible* environment."

Small, unforeseen details had the potential to decrease productivity in tiny but nonetheless significant ways. For example, office supplies like staplers were not stored in the cubicles, forcing employees to leave their desk when they needed to use one. Although a PC purchase program equipped many of the employees with laptop computers and the company paid for an extra phone line to be installed in the homes of the sales staff, the extent to which XYZ would subsidize or provide other necessities for a home office, such as new office furniture, was unclear. Because of the larger financial situation, the company was not always able to provide employees with the support they needed to ensure a stress-free transition with no loss of productivity.

The lack of support was seen in the mobile workers' lack of access to technological tools like printers but also to people and expertise. During this period, XYZ was in the midst of shifting its corpus of organizational knowledge and information from an analog paper-based system to digital files. For the first few months of the telework initiative, these paper-based files and binders had to be manually moved from place to place by sales staff because they were not yet digitized and available on the company Intranet. Teleworkers spoke of the nuisance of forgetting one file at home and having to turn around to retrieve it, and the transportation of heavy files and binders prompted one employee to complain she felt like a "pack mule." Two months later, this employee had shifted her schedule so that she worked primarily out of the office instead of her home. In an e-mail, she said she did this to "avoid the confusion of having two offices and forgetting stuff at one place or another and to save my back from schlepping tons of books and files back-n-forth [sic]." She added that "until the resources are ALL there, I prefer to do it this way."

An online survey was administered to Culver City employees in the late spring of 1997.[2] In response to an open-ended question about whether the respondent felt he or she had more control since the move, one employee wrote:

> The challenges are with the lack of resources in our homes. Some, like myself, are not equipped at this time with fax machine, second-business line, copiers, etc. . . . Of course the biggest hindrance is the lack of resources (i.e., copiers, printers, etc.) If that was made available, working full-time telecommuting would be a breeze and the time in the office would be substantially reduced.

At this point in time, the lack of technological support combined with the travel between two offices made it more difficult for some mobile workers to get the information they needed when they needed it. For instance, salespeople without fax machines in their homes had to travel to the office whenever they had to receive or send a fax. If they accidentally left a crucial page of the document at home, where the majority of their files were now located, they would have to drive home again. The goal of the initiative was to enable access to information regardless of location, but it was difficult to achieve this objective immediately, especially given the financial constraints of the organization.

Employees who did not have the luxury of an extra bedroom or home office experienced additional stress over the problem of finding a work space in the home. One employee had to move to a larger apartment; another initially tried to set up an office in a windowless garage with only one electrical outlet and no heat or air-conditioning. He then moved his office into a small back room in his house but had to keep all his files stored in the garage. He spoke wistfully of the access to files he had while working in the centralized office, noting that he had to buy a mobile phone so he could take it out to the garage to look for files while fielding calls. It was obviously not an optimal work environment.

ANAHEIM OFFICE TELEWORK PROGRAM

Approximately nine months after the Culver City office relocated and the organization had transitioned to a mobile work model, a similar move took place in the XYZ offices to the south. Until September 1997, XYZ maintained two offices in Orange County, one in Irvine and another in nearby Anaheim, approximately 20 minutes from Irvine via freeway.

The Anaheim office housed the national headquarters of XYZ. Since the Irvine branch office was slated for closure anyway, it was decided that it would be treated as a pilot study for a hoteling scheme that might be replicated elsewhere in the country. Reasons for this shift, as with Culver City, were multiple and varied: objectives of the Irvine/Anaheim pilot included increasing sales productivity and reducing real estate expense. It was also believed that successful salespeople did not need dedicated desks because they were in the field most of the time and mobilizing them would increase their "face time" with customers.

Other Comco offices across the country had implemented telework schemes on an individual basis prior to this—for instance, one employee in a Midwest territory was allowed to work from home to cover a particular region of the state—but nothing had been done on this scale. According to the vice president of human resources, "Southern California decided to go a little bit further."

Comco's newly formed telecommuting consulting business, SmartFocus, was commissioned to help with the transition to telecommuting and mobile officing. A SmartFocus analyst joined the project in early 1997 and suggested a hoteling scheme to XYZ's president, who was known to be an enthusiastic proponent of telecommuting. Earlier, he had mandated that each branch manager had to submit a plan to reduce office space when they approached the end of their building's lease, with the eventual goal of utilizing 50 percent less office space. The Anaheim office's adoption of telecommuting was clearly a result of his influence and "the telecommuting situation" was said to be his "child." Now, as a result, the shift to telecommuting in Anaheim that occurred with his explicit approval had more support, financial and therefore technological, than the earlier shift in Culver City.

After the Culver City office relocated to the smaller office, but before it was officially announced that the Irvine office would be closed down, the SmartFocus team administered a survey to employees at the three XYZ branches in Southern California at that time: Irvine, Culver City, and San Diego. This survey inquired about the home environment of employees in an attempt to ascertain whether they were good candidates for telecommuting. For example, one question asked whether the employee had small children at home. Other questions attempted to tap into employees' feelings about not having a dedicated work space and their expectations about the transition process.

Responses about how often employees used their assigned office were interpreted to suggest that many employees could make the transition to a telecommuting situation easily. Except for administrative personnel (who were in the office 100 percent of the time) and sales engineers (one of whom was in the office 100 percent of the time, and the others over half of the time), respondents reported that they were in their assigned offices only periodically. Respondents were asked to rate various schemes for reducing office space. When asked their preference, the majority of respondents indicated that their first choice would be to have a dedicated, reduced-size work space. Hoteling or offices assigned on a first come, first served basis was the second choice of most. The survey results, according to the company, indicated that all employees, with the exception of the operations managers, felt that they would make good candidates for telecommuting and that many employees felt that the dial-up capability of the network was too slow and needed upgrading.

In September 1997, the branch office in Irvine was closed, for financial and other reasons. The company went through a significant downsizing at this point—sometimes more positively referred to as "right-sizing." Some employees working out of Irvine were laid off or resigned. Although a "Virtual Office Procedure" training notebook distributed to employees emphasized that "[p]articipation in the virtual office program is voluntary," in essence sales associates and sales engineers had no options other than to be "virtualized." Some staff positions, such as an operations manager who felt he needed to be more available to coworkers than telecommuting would allow, were allowed to maintain a permanent office in the Anaheim facility. Others either telecommuted from home or adopted a flexible work schedule that combined working at the Anaheim office with working from a home office and client sites. As explained by the SmartFocus consultant, "If you chose to come into the office every day that was up to you, but you didn't have a dedicated space."

SmartFocus conducted training designed for those entering an "alternative workplace program" and made hardware and software recommendations. For instance, Hewlett Packard had recently introduced a combination color printer/fax/copier/scanner and SmartFocus recommended that the company provide these for the mobile worker's home use. The training covered issues of practical interest to teleworkers, such as how to organize a home office, schedule meeting rooms, apply for reimbursements, and other administrative details. In addition, an open discussion on how to manage by objectives was offered. According to the training schedule, 2 minutes were allotted to a discussion of "Virtual Office Co-worker Relations."

A postimplementation survey was administered by Smart-Focus in December 1997, about 3 months after the Irvine office was closed.[3] All employees, managers, and supervisors in the Culver City (Los Angeles) office, the Irvine office (now in Anaheim), and the San Diego office were approached, but response levels were low. The survey was designed to assess the effectiveness of the Anaheim virtual office environment and to locate the changes in work, socialization, and management styles that resulted from the shift to virtual work. The study reported that the Anaheim hoteling facilities were hardly utilized: one-third of the virtualized respondents claimed that they did not use the cubicles at all, and most others indicated that they used the space less than one full day a week. According to this survey, the purpose for coming into the office had shifted from performing administrative duties to fulfilling interpersonal needs, such as meeting with team members. On the postimplementation survey, half of the respondents mentioned that the cubicle area in Anaheim looked "demoralizing," "bad," or "uninviting."

At this time, the Anaheim office was in the process of being renovated. Prior to the pilot study and subsequent permanent transfer of the Irvine employees, the building was primarily a manufacturing plant. Located in an industrial area of Anaheim in the heart of Orange County, near the intersection of two freeways, the squat, nondescript building covers more area than a square city block. In front of it sprawls a parking lot, large enough to accommodate the Southern California habit of commuting alone to work. Prior to the virtualization project, the building housed approximately 375 employees in the areas of manufacturing, human resources, and finance.

The manufacturing area is a huge room, as large as a high school football field, full of people and technical equipment. The high ceilings, fluorescent lights, and open expanse give it an industrial feeling, in sharp contrast to the rather posh reception area. In the large lunchroom, Comco's Japanese influence can be seen most clearly: a Ping-Pong table sits among the vending machines and long tables, and Japanese motif posters and decorations hang on the walls. The employees at the plant are racially diverse, primarily Asians, Latinos, and whites. At lunch time, many in the cafeteria eat their meals from plastic containers they bring from home.

To reach the cubicles set aside for telecommuting employees, one must enter through a reception area and then walk down a hallway to the glass doors that open into the manufacturing area. Walking along the perimeter of the manufacturing area and down another hall leads one to the telecommuting offices: a row of six cubicles, each about 6 × 9 feet, with a standard-issue desk, a phone, and a tray of supplies such as paper clips and tape. According to the SmartFocus consultant, each employee is assigned a filing cabinet but most prefer to leave their materials at home. At one point it appeared as if someone had staked out his or her somewhat permanent territory with books and folders prominently displayed in one of the cubicles, but otherwise the cubicles were empty of any identifying decorations or personal artifacts save an organizational phone list tacked onto the wall.

In discussions about the move to Anaheim, a primary factor that many employees cited for their lack of enthusiasm regarding their new offices was the atmosphere of the Anaheim office. Salespeople described what they perceived to be unprofessional decor and a generally dreary, depressing environment. There was some discussion of plans to lease office space for the Anaheim/Irvine people to use until construction was completed on the Anaheim office, but this did not happen during the data collection period.

DEPARTURE OF A PRESIDENT AND CHANGES IN TELECOMMUTING POLICY

In December 1997, the president of the company, who had been a strong proponent of telework, stepped down (encouraged, possibly, by those above him). This position was not filled until August 1998, so the company functioned without an upper level of management for approximately 8 months. For much of this time, the Southern California sales division operated without a general manager or a sales manager. Salespeople were instructed to report to June O'Reilly, a regional vice president located in Phoenix, Arizona. This was obviously not an optimal arrangement, as O'Reilly was located out of state and was busy with a large territory that included Arizona and California. However, salespeople adapted to the change, using e-mail and phone calls to communicate with their supervisor.

In July 1998, approximately 7 months after O'Reilly took over, she sent out a voice-mail message to the sales staff, announcing that the telecommuting strategy was terminated and that all staff should plan to work out of the Anaheim office. She claimed this change would increase synergy and camaraderie among the staff. However, given the unpopularity of the Anaheim office and the fact that O'Reilly was still located in another state, this mandate was covertly ignored by many. For instance, one sales engineer used her voice-mail system to give the appearance of obeying orders while in reality maintaining her autonomy. She did not change her schedule, but rather rerecorded her voice-mail greeting, replacing "I am telecommuting today" with "I am away from my desk right now."

Soon afterward, it was announced that O'Reilly had left the company as well. The salespeople were told to report to the chief financial officer of the company, who was described as leaning more toward "old-school" management techniques and was opposed to telecommuting. However, in August 1998, XYZ announced the appointment of a new president and chief operating officer: Nancy Helms, an executive from a large and successful technology company.

CRAFTING A CULTURE: A NEW VISION FOR XYZ

Helms began her tenure with a round of talks to employees at the Anaheim office in which she introduced herself, spoke of her goals, and attempted to engineer an organizational culture.[4] In these talks, she presented her vision for XYZ with clearly outlined goals that included financial stability, building XYZ into a world-class organization, and raising customer and employee satisfaction. She also outlined her vision for the reengineering of XYZ's organizational culture. This new organizational culture was based on four basic tenets, which she enjoined the employees to embrace: Thirst to Learn, Winning Through Excellence, Walk the Talk, and Embrace Small Company Spirit (which included the admonition to "Make Work=Fun!!").

   Her speech focused on some of these ideas, such as thinking outside the box, embracing the concept of "stretch," and
the importance of the "learning organization." The organizational culture she described was a unified, learning organization in which people treated one another with respect and
honesty and were not afraid to think "outside the box" or to
"stretch." Many of these qualities fell under the rubric of what
she called the "small company spirit." One of the initiatives
that seemed to catch the audience's attention was the an-
nouncement that the "moose" would be "surfaced" whenever
someone violated these principles. By this, she meant dis-
playing to the guilty party either a stuffed toy moose or a picture of a moose. "Don't think it's dorky!" she scolded the
crowd, which got laughs. She suggested that at every meeting's end, in addition to reviewing the action points, employees would also recount situations in which the moose was
raised, why it was raised, and how to avoid it in the future.
She noted that a moose was brought to the meeting that
morning and was indeed raised. This was Helms's plan to
make change "fun."
   During her presentation, Helms used a rhetorical strategy
in which she simultaneously identified herself as both a recent
outsider and one who was now part of—indeed, leading—the
XYZ team. She discussed her goal of giving the audience an
"outsider's perspective" on Comco's strengths, and spoke
openly about her tenure at a major telephony and technology
company, mentioning that her friends at one of Comco's com-
petitors were "jealous" of some of Comco's products. Early in
her talk, she offered the caveat that many of the ideas in her
speech concerning Comco's problems and strengths were
based on conversations with others, so people should not be
"bashful" about telling her where she was wrong. For instance,
each of Helms's talks opened with an anecdote about her recent return from a trip to Japan where she had met with the
top management of the company, the "Japanese who's who."
The message they gave her, which she proceeded to dissemi-
nate at each meeting, was to "get the financials in check." In
this sense, although she was the bearer of both criticism of the
organization and bad news, it was not perceived as originating
directly from her.
   The response to Helms seemed quite positive. Among the
women sales staff, the fact that a woman was hired for such an
important position was cause for celebration. They also expressed

some surprise that a traditional Japanese organization would hire a woman for such a high-level position.

Changing Work Roles and Management Structure at Xyz

The XYZ team was accustomed to functioning within a specific hierarchical chain of command. However, when the two positions directly above the account manager—a sales manager and a general manager—were vacant for several months, sales representatives reported to a regional manager located in another state. This situation impacted the organizational culture as well as the salespeople's productivity. When asked about the effects of this management shift, one XYZ salesperson said, "It becomes very difficult to see that anything gets done, because I basically have all the responsibility and none of the authority." The employee went on to explain:

> What value I see in a general manager or a sales manager is usually a general manager can make a decision. And . . . rather quickly . . . a sales manager can usually pull things through the company and through other departments for you. That's their role, whereas the regional can't really do that. I mean they can tell someone to do something but they don't really have the time to follow up on it and see that it happens.

This employee indicated that she did not feel she needed a sales manager as much as a general manager, who would have the power to push things through. The sales representatives are all seasoned salespeople, she said, who do not need direct supervision as much as they need a person in charge who can make sure things happen on a timely basis.

In addition, XYZ was undergoing another shift in structure, this one prompted in part by the changing role of technology in the office environment. The role of secretaries and administrative assistants has changed with the influx of less expensive and more intuitive office technologies (Webster, 1996). Executives who previously dictated letters to be typed and proofread by secretaries now type their own letters and screen their own calls. This trend can also be seen at XYZ, where administrative support for salespeople diminished.

The move to the "mobile office" also had the effect of changing job functionalities. Because the sales representatives and the sales engineers were no longer co-located, salespeople were less likely to go to sales engineers for help and instead became more self-reliant. This self-reliance enabled the sales engineers to focus on their skills rather than supporting the sales representatives. The decrease in support staff also changed the way in which account managers did their jobs. Ironically, this decrease in support was termed "empowerment" by management, an odd turn of phrase that filtered down to the sales staff. As one salesperson explained:

> We've been empowered. That means that things we counted on in the past [that] a sales secretary would do: key in proposals, prepare PowerPoint presentations—three years ago you told a sales secretary [to do] what you wanted because you didn't have a computer. They did all that for you. Now through empowerment you do that yourself. There is no one to do those things for you.

She went on to clarify that this was a problem because when:

> I go back to what I'm paid to do—we have sales engineers that are supposed to be experts in configuring systems, pricing them, etc. Anything that you specialize in you can become very expedient in. But if you are a jack-of-all-trades, you get *kind of* good at everything, which is what I equate with what happened with the salespeople. Because [when] our focus is on learning products better, learning the switch better from a technical standpoint . . . that takes away from selling time.

In this case, the salesperson was resisting the redefinition of her job because she felt that it was not time effective for her to be responsible for areas outside her area of expertise. Becoming a generalist would take time away from what she was trained (and paid) to do: sell. Essentially, she felt that becoming a jack-of-all-trades was inefficient and reduced her ability to focus on closing sales—and, most likely, her commission.

For the salesperson, being asked to take responsibility for the technical aspects of pricing and selling took time away from what she was trained to do: close deals. However, from the perspective of the sales engineer, the shift was welcome. As one sales engineer said:

> Since we've been telecommuting the salespeople now look things up on their own before they'll call us because they

can't yell over our cubicle or whatever, so they're becoming more familiar and more technical on their own which means that we can take our responsibilities a step further also with the products."

In this case, the lack of geographical proximity among colleagues in different disciplines changed the nature of their job duties. The fact that sales representatives now "looked things up on their own" allowed the sales engineer to focus on higher level job responsibilities and to take her expertise "a step further." Both of these participants resisted becoming generalists. This case is especially interesting because it runs counter to much of the rhetoric surrounding the virtual office, in which employees welcome control over the entire work process. The trend away from traditional work roles and practices is said to be giving workers the "opportunity to earn more and to control their work situations" (Halal, 1996). This paradigm shift is breaking large controlling organizations into small, self-directed teams of knowledge workers that are "given almost total control—from product design to manufacturing, sales, service, and disposal" (Halal, 1996). However, as this case suggests, the question remains as to whether employees would rather be responsible for the entire work cycle ("empowered") or focus instead on the elements of the process tied directly to their training, compensation, and expertise.

Shaping Technology to Support Telecommuting

Management generally acknowledged that XYZ had "stumbled" in their transition to telecommuting. Two especially problematic areas had plagued the company since the Culver City experiment: a slow server that made accessing data a tedious process, and the fact that XYZ employees were not outfitted with the technology they needed to properly do their jobs. Slow servers and less-than-optimal communications technology not only created productivity lapses but also brought down morale.

All technology fails at one moment or another. However, when a massive change at the level of XYZ's shift to telecommuting takes place, there are bound to be many frustrations and technical problems. When SmartFocus did an analysis of the calls made to XYZ's Help Desk during the move to telework, they found that the average number of calls to the Help Desk more than doubled during the pilot period, when employees were attempting to set up home offices, access the network remotely, and install new software and hardware. When the Irvine office transitioned to mobile work, technical assistance calls went from 5 every two weeks to 22 in the same time period. The fact that these calls declined, although network problems had not been resolved, was interpreted by SmartFocus to indicate "virtual staff are resolving to live with problems rather than continue to ask for help."

XYZ employees showed creativity and resolve in adapting the technology to their needs by creating temporary work-arounds and bricolage-type solutions to technical problems. For example, one sales engineer who had long and lengthy problems with her e-mail account simply stopped using the corporate account and instead used her personal account from a private service provider for company correspondence. When she needed information from the company's Intranet, her sales engineer would download the information and send it to her personal e-mail account. In this way, the sales representative was able to get the information she needed while avoiding the problems associated with the computer network. Another example of this type of renegotiation is the employee who changed the outgoing message on her voice mail to rhetorically create a situation mandated by her supervisors, meanwhile changing little about her actual work habits.

The slow speed of remote access to the company network was generally acknowledged to be a problem, and in fact, several employees remarked that if they needed to download a large file they would go to the Anaheim facility rather than do it remotely. (Broadband connections were not available to employees at this time.) However, progress had been made in transferring analog files to digital ones that could be stored on and accessed from the network. This was in direct contrast to the early implementation of telecommuting at XYZ's Culver City office, where most information had been stored in analog binders that had to be carried from location to location.

XYZ Systems' Organizational Culture

To an outsider, the culture of XYZ Systems appears disjointed and diffuse, with pockets of subcultures and a lack of cohesion. Some of the employees associated the fragmented culture of the firm with its lack of a geographical locus. The removal of the organization's geographical center may have triggered the participants to give more symbolic credence to issues of space and location. In some ways, the employees looked toward the environment created for them by the company as an indication of the extent to which they were valued by the organization. For example, one salesperson described the difficulty in working in the Anaheim office:

> [In] the cubicle area, right now there's this big fan that blows over the first two cubicles and makes it hard to hear and is also a distraction and the acoustics are real bad, if someone is sitting in the cubicle next to you. . . . It's loud. I mean people can start having a conversation two cubicles down and I can be having a conversation with you and all of a sudden it's like I'm hearing them like they're in my ear. And it looks like crap. We're going out [representing] ourselves as this $36 billion company and we feel like little orphans. . . . Because we're in sales. We have to feel good. . . . You have to feel like you're a million bucks. That's why they say, dress for success, etc. Your environment has to be created to exude that as well.

Here, the salesperson is looking to her physical environment to support her representation of herself to her clients as working for an organization that is a "global leader" and a "$36 billion company." This is in contrast, she seems to feel, to the image exemplified by the cubicles given to the salespeople, where "it looks like a company that's not doing as well. . . . I mean there are stains and stuff on the cubicles."A sales engineer complained about the high warehouse ceilings and the general lack of maintenance:

> At least they could bring the ceilings down to make it look like an office environment! You know, I sat down [at] one of the desks the other day and went to put my PC laptop on it and the top of the desk started coming off! I go "Yeah, I'll come in here and sit in this mess." No way! And half the jacks for your PCs and all, they don't work. There's nobody that checks them. I'm going to come in here? And work in this mess? When I've got a really great office at home that's fully operational? I don't think so!

In contrast, the Irvine office was described by a salesperson as "perfect":

Irvine was perfect. They should never have taken us out of there. It was perfect. We had a little lunchroom, we had a library, we had our desks of course and everything, parking was right out front, very convenient to stores and stuff like that. [It was close to my house.] It was perfect . . . and I liked working there the first time too, I really enjoyed it. I felt like . . . it was a very warm feeling. When I went back in there I felt like I was home again.

This feeling was lost in the movement to the Anaheim office. Further adding to the confusion that marked XYZ for much of the period of this study was the company's lack of leadership at the top management levels. This was discussed by one salesperson during a discussion about Comco's productivity. The employee brought up the mission statement, explaining:

I think they're on the right track in terms of our one paragraph capability statement. . . . Most people are like "That sounds good, but what do you mean?" But what it does mean is that we can take a customer who may be global and allow that customer . . . to communicate quicker, get information out to people faster, which helps them stay ahead of their competition. We can provide techniques or technology that will help them take care of their customers better. And I think all the pieces are there. What we need to do is just get someone in the lead that says, "Okay, gang, this is how we're going to do it." And . . . be solid in that and confident in that.

Here, the employee attributes the problem to the lack of a "solid" and "confident" leader who could mobilize the group. Possibly because the company lacked stability, it was unable to quickly adapt to the changing business environment. Seasoned salespeople, who were used to a layer of management that could facilitate and direct, were forced to operate in a vacuum of authority. However, they also "made do" in times of need, as indicated in the following statement of a sales engineer:

[A salesperson] and I were working on a bid a couple of weeks ago. You know, couldn't find [the regional vice president]. Didn't have a sales manager. What we would normally go to a sales manager for . . . no sales manager, or GM, or [regional vice president]. On margin decisions and legal things . . . we did it ourselves! Made 'em up.

What are they going to do? We get the deal . . . it's not a matter of well, you don't bid it because you don't have anyone. You do the best you can. And they know that we're doing that.

In contrast to iLAN, XYZ employees are extremely cognizant of the chain of command. So, although they might joke about not knowing their job responsibilities, for the most part XYZ employees were performing roles that were well defined. For example, when asked about his job duties, an operations manager first joked about not knowing, but then went on to give a succinct and coherent explanation of the organizational structure and his specific place in it.

Because XYZ originally operated as a traditional organization (both geographically and in its use of hierarchical structure), the transition to telework resonated differently than it might for an organization that was virtual from inception. In particular, the highly structured bureaucracy made it difficult for employees to fulfill their job functions when key positions were not filled. Of course, it is hard to determine which of these problems were associated with the adoption of telework and which were linked to other changes in the organization, such as the loss of a president or the larger financial environment. In the following two chapters, the way in which telework was socially shaped in the home and the organization will be described, drawing on the cases of iLAN Systems and XYZ.

Chapter Five

Telework and the Organization: Changing Patterns of Management, Work, and Socialization

As the two cases suggest, telework reorganizes traditional managerial and organizational structures, but these changes are not independent of preexisting structural, technological, geographical, and cultural tendencies. In many of these arenas, a similar dynamic emerged: telework reinforced preexisting trends and dynamics, and teleworkers used ICTs in ways that were consistent with existing patterns of communication and work. These findings can best be understood through a social shaping perspective, which acknowledges that a technology such as telework creates the *potential* for social change, which is enacted by individuals and organizations. In other words, technology creates both constraints and possibilities, which are then realized or not, depending on the actions of individuals.

STRUCTURE: DIFFERENCES IN ORGANIZATIONAL AND TELEWORK ADOPTION

To understand telework's implications at each firm, it is important to understand the structural differences between iLAN Systems and XYZ that undoubtedly affected the way telework was instantiated at each firm. In some ways, iLAN's flatter, more fluid organization seemed to be better suited to a mobile work style than XYZ's more hierarchical, rigid one. iLAN's organizational structure, which was designed to be geographically decentralized from inception, was a good fit with the decentralized organizational geography encouraged by telework.

A second structural characteristic that may have enabled iLAN to incorporate telework elegantly lies in its somewhat autocratic structure wherein the founders made most of the high-level decisions and assigned employees tasks based on the situation at hand, rather than the less fluid assignment of tasks seen at XYZ. This "wheel" communication network de-emphasized the need for constant communication among employees. Additionally, although sometimes iLAN's technicians worked in tandem to solve a particular network issue, the type of work was not as dependent on meetings, teams, and group activities as other professions, such as advertising. Because many engineers worked autonomously or with only one of the founders, the loss of spontaneous, effortless face-to-face communication among peers was not as disruptive as it might have been in other circumstances.

The structure of XYZ, which is quite different from iLAN's, also affected the ways in which telework was shaped by the organization and its members. In many ways, the telework initiative at XYZ could be considered successful—for instance, many of the sales staff expressed satisfaction with the flexibility it afforded—but its relative success was restricted by the organization's management structure. Members of the sales staff showed creativity and resolve in solving problems, technical and otherwise. However, it was also clear that salespeople were hampered by the lack of autonomy they were granted by the management structure in concert with the lack of direction that resulted from the organization's unfilled leadership positions.

In addition, other structural factors such as differences in organizational leadership and size had an impact on how telework was adopted at each organization.

DIFFERENCES IN STRUCTURE: ORGANIZATIONAL FOUNDERS AND LEADERS

The founder of an organization has the potential to have a major impact on an organization's culture (Schein, 1985). This aspect of organizational culture is important to consider in regard to both cases. iLAN System's founders were personally well-known to all employees, and meeting their expectations was obviously a high priority. XYZ, on the other hand, was created through the merger of three traditionally structured companies, all of whom were connected to one Japanese parent company. Whereas most iLAN employees interacted in some fashion with one of the founders on a daily basis, very few if any XYZ employees, besides the top management, interacted with the Japanese forefathers of the organization or had any immediate or personal knowledge of them.

Leadership was another important aspect of each organization. XYZ was without a president for approximately 8 months, a situation acknowledged by many to be challenging. The critical need for top management was made evident by one employee's comment that "What we need to do is just get someone in the lead that says, 'Okay, gang, this is how we're going to do it.'" In comparison, iLAN had a leadership team consisting of two leaders, one of whom was highly regarded as a technician and the other who was described by a support employee as a "visionary who's thinking about directions and paths and stuff."

Complicating this situation was the fact that XYZ's telecommuting initiative was spearheaded by its president, who had the power to allocate technical and financial resources. While this resulted in solid financial support while he was in office, his departure from the company created a vacuum of support for the program. This hobbled financial resources for telecommuting and may have created confusion on the part of employees as to the overall organizational strategy and direction regarding the mobile work initiative. In contrast to this, iLAN proudly identified itself as a virtual company, as indicated by the oft-told story of the client who showed up at the Mail Boxes Etc. store and the fact that the president had written a book on the subject. iLAN employees felt comfortable and supported in their role as mobile employees.

DIFFERENCES IN STRUCTURE: HIERARCHY VERSUS FLEXIBILITY, AGE, AND SIZE

Another key difference lies in the fact that XYZ's organizational scheme was fairly traditional and hierarchical, whereas iLAN Systems' organizational structure was more flexible, especially in terms of the roles employees were willing to play. For instance, iLAN employees answered phones if others were busy, whereas XYZ salespeople were less willing to complete work not directly applicable to their particular sales goals (and, hence, commissions). In these cases, existing norms about the organization's structure may have influenced the employees' ability to flourish in a less structured telework environment. Because XYZ was fairly hierarchical, salespeople found it difficult to adjust to an environment where several gaps in the organizational chart remained unfilled.

At iLAN, employees were fairly comfortable operating in a less structured organizational environment. As one support employee explained, iLAN is a "very flat structure; basically there's no bureaucracy . . . and it's certainly a less formal environment. . . . It's a more fluid environment where what you're doing and what your responsibilities are can change very rapidly depending on the situation and you have to be ready for that, compared to [another company] where you've got your area that you're working in and there are the other areas that are formally boxed off."

Because iLAN employees knew they would be working in a geographically distributed environment from the time they were hired, the transition to telework was not as stressful as it may have been for XYZ employees. As one iLAN support employee stated, "It's based on working out of your home, so you kind of know what you're getting into." At iLAN, employees self-selected the company and therefore the telework mode. XYZ employees, in contrast, joined an organization with a traditional structure which then "went virtual." The majority were not offered a choice about whether or not to telework, and indeed, when asked about the option in surveys, expressed the desire for a permanent, albeit small, dedicated work space as opposed to a mobile office. Although many organizations may not have the luxury of including employee input on major decisions such as whether to adopt nontraditional work arrangements, it seems clear that the transition to telecommuting is less stressful for employees when they self-select this mode of work.

The size and age of the organizations also influenced their structure and culture. Because iLAN is much smaller than XYZ, it is easier for organization members to know one another. Indeed, this feeling may be what the new president of XYZ attempted to capture in her organizational culture mandates crafted to instill a "small company" feeling. The size of iLAN undoubtedly enabled a decentralized structure that would have been difficult to maintain at a larger organization. Additionally, the fact that iLAN is a relatively young organization also affected the culture of the organization. Although participants came to iLAN with expectations, informed by previous work environments, the entrepreneurial founders at iLAN encouraged the notion that this was a new, fresh organizational structure in which long-standing organizational dictums, like the need for meetings, were questioned. The lack of a central office only reinforced this interpretation. In contrast, XYZ is a larger, more established firm with entrenched organizational norms, which probably made the transition to a new work arrangement more challenging.

TECHNOLOGY: CHANGING THE WAY ORGANIZATIONS WORK

Information and communication technologies both enabled and constrained how organizational members did their jobs and how the organization as a whole functioned. For both the engineers and the salespeople, technology was an integral part of how these teleworkers worked. However, there were also differences in both individual and organizational access to technology: access to the tools themselves and the expertise needed to fully utilize them. Exploring these differences offers us lessons for future telework implementations—primarily, the critical nature of adequate technical support and network access for mobile workers.

Members of both organizations used ICTs to retrieve, organize, and process information. The movement from analog to digital files was, especially for members of XYZ's sales staff, linked to a larger shift in work practices, and access to networked information was sometimes problematic, although employees were creative in finding solutions.

In the early stages of the telework initiative, XYZ employees were hampered by the fact that they had to carry around heavy folders and papers in order to have access to critical information, such as technical specifications and pricing standards. Because some employees did not have access to certain technological tools (such as fax machines) in their home offices, their dependence on analog information constrained them—both figuratively and literally. One employee dramatized this issue by claiming that she felt like a "pack mule."

Contrary to the rhetoric of the virtual office, in which proponents claim geography will become obsolete, geographical issues took on greater importance when XYZ shifted to a mobile work environment. It was simply not possible to forget about geography because the process of maintaining multiple work spaces and transporting analog files became a hindrance. For instance, employees who worked both in the office and at home had to identify, gather, and transport any folders, files, or books they might need that day. Not having a fax machine in the home meant driving to the office or to the local copy store, entailing out-of-pocket expenses for employees. Reliance on paper-based files had negative repercussions for the organizations as well, because they took the chance of losing valuable or irreplaceable information to theft, fire, or carelessness when employees kept business files in home offices or, in one case, a garage.

As more materials were either digitized or created in digital form, problems of geographical access were replaced by problems of technological access. At XYZ, as more information was made available on the company Intranet, many of the shared folders and binders became obsolete. However, the digital format was accompanied by access problems of a different order. Specifically, the network server that contained the data was slow and difficult to access over modems linked to telephone lines. Even so, though, the shift to digitized information seemed to bring XYZ closer to realizing the original vision of the "mobile worker."

At iLAN, employees did not speak of technology in terms of a time-based shift from analog to digital, but rather spoke more generally about the different paradigms of work that accompanied analog and digital information. For instance, a former iLAN support employee spoke of the ease with which digital information could be manipulated and shared, as compared to paper-based information, using her current work environment as an example:

> I've got some paper copies of some stuff—there are certain things I have to turn in on paper. Occasionally I bring home some papers to look at. I hate that! I don't like papers. I really enjoy doing stuff on the computer. . . . This thing [referring to a paper form], if I make a mistake I've got to erase it by hand and all that. If this whole block of paragraph is wrong I've got to redo it. This was given to me in this form—it says "Tell me about your work units"—the lady gave me this and said "What is it changing to?" and I wrote what it was changing to, and I've got to write why it changed. She didn't give it to me in digital form although she could have e-mailed it to me. Maybe next year I'll bug her about it and say "Give it to me on e-mail." . . . I have to hand transcribe this figure into this document. The computer is better! The less I get on paper the more I like it!

Other employees reinterpreted information and communication technologies, using them in new ways to either get around problems or to shape the technology to meet their needs. For instance, one iLAN support employee used email to structure and organize his work (a ready-made to do list), rather than just as a means to communicate with others:

When you get a voice mail and you don't want to work on that item right away, what do you do? You get out a piece of paper and a pencil and . . . ?

INTERVIEWER: You write it down.

And pencil and paper, pardon the expression, *sucks.* It's a lot easier with e-mail because it's all written down. You can even check e-mail at a time when you can deal with that stuff. Or you can check it eight times a day like we do. And just not act on something because—there's your to do list. You just pull up your e-mail and there are the seven things you got today. Now you can deal with these things. Or, you know what? You're not going to deal with them now, you'll deal with them with your first cup of coffee in the morning.

Gladwell (2002) examines recent literature on some of the critical differences between analog and digital information—namely, the ways in which paper is superior to the computer for certain types of tasks. For instance, air traffic controllers still use pieces of paper, not a computer, to chart planes in flight. Examining the fundamental question of why paper sales have continued to rise during the supposed preeminence of the "paperless office," Gladwell cites the opinions of cognitive psychologists and ergonomics experts who argue that for certain tasks, piles of paper work just as well as, if not better than, digital files. Gladwell reiterates Sellen and Harper's (2001) argument, which is that paper's flexibility, tangibility, and tailorability make it uniquely qualified to support collaborative work (in which a document is passed around a group of colleagues and annotated). In these case studies, a distinct desire to be "paperless" was a large part of the dominant organizational rhetoric, and employees were clearly trying to adopt this attitude.

The social shaping approach to technology use speaks to this reshaping of technology by users as an expected and natural occurrence. It is important to remember that technology is imbued with notions about users' desires, needs, and abilities. ILAN's NetNag software, designed to help manage telecommuters, exemplifies the thesis forwarded by Woolgar (1996) and others who embrace the social shaping approach to technology, which is that "technology is society made durable" (Woolgar, 1996, p. 90). Because software designers embed notions of social relations into the technology they design, conceptions of intended users—their capabilities, desires, job tasks, even the extent to which they can be trusted not to sabotage the system—influence the way in which a particular product is designed to function.[1] This can clearly be seen in the design and description of NetNag as included in the book produced by iLAN. NetNag is "a computer application that helps an organization identify work to be done, monitor its progress and assist in the management of it's [sic] entire work effort" (Reynolds & Brusseau, 1998, p. 155). NetNag allows for various tasks to be assigned to responsible parties in the organization, enabling a focus on "managing the work, not the worker." The software prompts technicians to complete projects that may get overlooked when something "hot" comes in, but need to be done nonetheless. In addition, each task can be configured so that the assignee is routinely asked for e-mail status reports. As described by one iLAN employee, if a task is slated to take a month, and if at every weekly status request the employee confirms progress, then at the end of that period, the task should be done. In this way, the software deflects attention from the employee completing the task to the task itself, according to the designers.

Similarly, by forcing managers to prioritize work and assign tasks, the software enforces what many researchers see as a managerial prerequisite for successful telecommuting, the shift from observing activity to assessing results. Unfortunately, this is not often the case. Few of the organizations included in Kurland and Egan's (1999) study used assessment strategies in which telecommuters were evaluated on observable and measurable outcomes, as recommended by the literature on the topic. According to Reynolds and Brusseau (1998), NetNag ostensibly "avoids a situation, [sic] where a manager who [sic] refuses to prioritize tasks or onerous-to-produce reports. In such an instance, a manager uses his position of power in the organization to avoid managing. He dumps everything on the employee who is forced to make choices without guidance. This sets the employee up to be the fall guy for anything that doesn't get accomplished" (p. 157).

In the case of NetNag, the software is assumed, indeed engineered, to have an influence on the way in which managers delegate work. iLAN created NetNag to govern the behavior of its employees and to compensate for problematic supervisory habits often seen in telework relationships. At iLAN, one of the secondary functions of the NetNag software was to capture and distribute organizational knowledge about work processes. It was hoped this information would be used to identify improvements to work processes and orient new staff (Reynolds & Brusseau, 1998, p. 158). However, employees differed in the extent to which they used the database, and its utility for the transfer of organizational knowledge was unclear.

Critical organizational knowledge—information about clients, sales strategies, gossip—has traditionally been shared through spontaneous and informal interactions when employees are co-located (Brown & Duguid, 2000). Digitizing analog information or codifying tacit knowledge entails tedious documentation efforts on the part of employees, for which there is often little compensation. Moreover, the historical precedence of using face-to-face communication to exchange potentially sensitive information is strong. Once information is digitized and codified, there needs to be a system in place for locating it, if it is to be utilized. In analog office environments, the location of certain files have traditionally been communicated informally as well as through formal means. Participants in this study discussed the importance of spontaneous, informal communication—such as overhearing someone in another cubicle discussing a problem and offering a solution—and its role in facilitating the transfer of valuable organizational knowledge. The importance of this kind of "incidental learning" has been discussed in other contexts (Brown & Duguid, 2000).

Some of the problems surrounding organizational knowledge and technology were illustrated by the case of one creative XYZ salesperson who, for one of her projects, created an electronic database into which other members of the organization could contribute contact information and other data. She sent out an e-mail that directed her colleagues to the online form and asked them to complete it. She explained that her colleagues seemed uncomfortable with sharing information this way and preferred to speak with her directly:

> I got back [a voice-mail message that said] "I have this customer name, and they're doing this, but call me!" [Laughter] And that's fine, except it's not what I needed. Remember that form? What I really needed was for you to fill that out! And then at the bottom of that you could say, call me, because I really don't want you to call this customer until I talk to you or whatever it is you want to convey. So I end up calling them back and finally you know after a few voice mails pulling up their e-mail and filling out the form myself. [Laughter].

In this case, habitual ways of sharing information among salespeople—ephemeral forms of communication such as face to face or telephone—were not easily replaced. As this example suggests, the introduction of a new technology alone will not create social change—the technology needs to mirror, amplify, or reflect an underlying social tendency or truth. In this case, the existence of a database alone was not enough to convince this employee's colleagues to change their old habits about exchanging sensitive information via ephemeral forms of communication, rather than documenting it in an electronic format.

The effects of new ICTs on the process of sharing organizational knowledge can be seen most clearly in the case of a small firm like iLAN. Heavy utilization of ICTs allowed the small firm to capitalize fully on the knowledge base of its employees. For instance, the company claimed a knowledge base of multiple programming languages and various kinds of expertise; in reality, perhaps only one engineer was fluent in a specific programming language. However, because any engineer could tap into the knowledge base of his or her coworkers, iLAN's ability to troubleshoot software problems was vastly increased.

In an obvious but often-overlooked implementation reality, information or knowledge is useless unless it can be accessed by the individuals that need it, when they need it. The fact that XYZ was finally able to digitize sales materials and put them online was a moot point if no one could access the server. In the case of knowledge held by individuals, these individuals need to be accessible by others if the knowledge is to be put to use. For instance, iLAN's database listing each engineer and his area of expertise was useless if the engineer was unavailable for consultation. As one of the founders explained, "We also have these Nextel phones so if you don't know the answer to a problem you can beep somebody who does. For example, everybody may not know Filemaker Pro, maybe one or two people know Filemaker Pro, but they can get in touch with somebody who knows it." Although, as he went on to note, this strategy only works when the technology itself works; if the employee was out of range, then his or her expertise and knowledge base was not available to others in the organization and essentially rendered worthless.

Even if organizational knowledge and information is codified in digital form and this information has the potential to be physically accessed (e.g., the server is up; all employees are in cell phone range), a third issue involves whether employees in a distributed environment are able to locate the information they need. That is, do they know what information is where? In traditional office environments, tracking and finding analog files is done in multiple ways, through informal conversation and formal placement. Teleworkers mentioned situations in the traditional office environment in which spontaneous, informal communication—such as overhearing someone in another cubicle talking about a certain strategy or problem—resulted in the transfer of valuable organizational knowledge. These types of informal communication scenarios are less frequent in distributed work environments. As an iLAN engineer explained, the problem with transfer of knowledge in a distributed work setting is that informal communication is constrained: "If the employee isn't there, if he can't pick up the stuff by osmosis around the watercooler from other employees who happen to have had that job function previously, how's he going to get his information?"

Similarly, an XYZ salesperson explained:

> It's just like in the office. Because we are together people feel like, "Hey, I know Patti was working on something where she gave the customer an executive summary that talked about this, this and this. I'm going to go ask Patti. You know she has that . . . file and can give it to me." Because I might have stuff just on the server but guess what, it's under "PATTIFILE"—nobody cares what's under my file on the server because it's my file. But [there] might be some great stuff there. If I'm in the office and I overhear a conversation that's in the next cubicle, I might say, "I got something on that!" See, that kind of interchange you can't have with e-mail or voice mail.

This sort of spontaneous exchange of information is less common in a dispersed work environment, because ICTs cannot currently replicate the social learning that occurs when co-located employees inadvertently overheard one another's frustrations, challenges, and solutions. Although electronic databases have some benefits in this regard (such as the ability to tap into a much wider network of experts and to store and filter information), they also require action on the part of the solution provider and the solution seeker, in contrast to the more passive and indiscriminate knowledge-sharing available to co-located individuals.

A second benefit of co-location and face-to-face communication is that it enables one to gauge a potential interactant's receptiveness (or lack thereof) to communication. In certain professions, such as computer programming, interrupting someone in the midst of a complicated task can be disastrous. For this reason, the telephone—with its insistence on immediate attention and its ineffective ability to indicate "Do Not Disturb"—is a poor replacement for face-to-face communication in some contexts. However, ICTs such as instant messaging, especially when paired with broadband "always on" network access, show promise in this respect. A quick instant message to a colleague who has indicated he or she is receptive to communication (through the system's status setting) could replicate this kind of quick, simple transaction without the drain on attention a phone call at an inopportune time might entail.

As one XYZ salesperson explained:

> You know, you had asked me before, well, if you're telecommuting, is that doing something to your social culture, with the peers that you work with? Yeah, because you're not learning what they're winning from. You're just out there on your own. Well, having a sales manager can kind of help you, but if you figure they're going out on calls with five or six people when they get with you, they're just trying to get through your calls. They don't want to spend time talking to you about what Sally's doing and what Tom's doing and what worked for them, and "Sam over here, he did this and boy, did that really mess up his sale." They're not thinking like that, but when we're together. . . . That's why I said, I don't know what the magic number is, I don't think we have to see each other every day, but I think that periodically you have to allow people that work together to collaborate, because we all grow from that.

How does one "learn from what others are winning from" in a dispersed environment? The question of whether technology can replicate informal communication in this sense is unresolved. For instance, gossip traditionally communicates valuable organizational information, but most people are uncomfortable communicating gossip via e-mail. However, between two trusted friends, e-mail might be used to communicate a wide range of topics and information. As illustrated by these cases, technical solutions alone will not work in the absence of necessary structural and cultural elements, such as trust.

SOCIAL SHAPING OF TECHNOLOGY:
INDIVIDUAL AND ORGANIZATIONAL VARIATIONS

Within these organizations, a great deal of variation was observed in regard to participants' technological strategies and attitudes. For instance, one salesperson spent hours trying to access her organizational e-mail account from home, but eventually gave up and just adopted a work-around—an e-mail account from her ISP. In other cases, employees put in extra hours to master a new software package. Individuals differed widely in their experience with and enthusiasm for the use of ICTs.

Unequal access to ICTs—both knowledge and hardware—was also seen at the organizational level, where there were substantial differences in the two organizations' ability to provide technological support. In general, iLAN tended to invest heavily in technological tools. In one case, the organization paid for installation of an ISDN line into the home of one employee who did not necessarily need or want it. XYZ, because of the larger financial environment, could not provide its entire sales staff with the tools they needed to do their jobs effectively and efficiently. The fact that XYZ telecommuters were not fully supported technically during some phases of telework's introduction affected some teleworkers' productivity and morale. For instance, in an early interview (April 1997), one salesperson explained, "We are quasi telecommuting. We can because we are allowed to, but we can't because we aren't given the resources. For example, if you leave a file at home—that part that I'm finding to be a true difficulty. The idea of telecommuting is fabulous. If I had all the resources here I would be so productive. . . . I would be worried that I would be a workaholic."

Over a year later, an XYZ manager echoed these themes when he explained:

> We aren't that sophisticated here at XYZ yet and so it's more cumbersome for people to work at home, it's slower for them to get on the network and get files and things like that. . . .
>
> As a company we just aren't that sophisticated yet. . . . My wife has a laptop made by the company she works for, so if her laptop isn't working, she just gives it back to them and they give her another one all fully loaded

ready to go. Where here it's like pulling teeth to get them to do something with it because it's going to cost us. And so we're watching those expenses.

These comments indicate the importance of adequately supporting teleworkers technically. However, this support has to be structural as well as technical. For instance, these employees are referring to two different aspects of technical support—the importance of having accessible, digital files (the data) and the need for functioning hardware and servers (the means by which to access the data). Both of these elements need to be addressed simultaneously, at a high level of the organization. Localized changes—such as giving employees laptops but not digitizing the data they need to access—will be inadequate.

Some of the differences in organizational support may be due to the fact that iLAN was started by and run by engineers, whereas for XYZ employees, technology was more peripheral. It facilitated their work processes but did not have the exulted status it did among the engineers of iLAN. Most of iLAN's engineers, clearly, were extremely excited by the technology—in a sense, it represented more than just their job, it was their raison d'être, and therefore they were more willing to engage in technical problem-solving.

GEOGRAPHY AND THE CULTURE OF THE ORGANIZATION

The introduction of telework arrangements alters the geography of the organization in many ways, only some of which are visible to observers. The architecture, layout, and design of an organization's office are important because they communicate information to both internal and external constituents. In trying to gain insights into an organization's culture, researchers look to the organization's physical manifestation as an important window into what the organization values, how it presents itself to outsiders, and other important characteristics.[2] For teleworkers who spend little time at a centralized office surrounded by peers, these organizational cues may be muted.

Many buildings are designed specifically to identify the organization as having certain characteristics, such as innovativeness, conservatism, or environmental awareness. A building's design and architecture can communicate the extent of the organization's financial health, its attitude toward traditionalism, espoused corporate values, and other elements of its organizational identity. The architecture may be purely functional (for instance, Bentham's panopticon) or it may be a public relations hook (for example, Chiat-Day's innovative Venice offices, designed by Frank Gehry). Its address alone can speak volumes, as indicated by the bloated value of an address on Wall Street. In *Cyberlane Commuter*, iLAN uses its lack of a corporate address as a rhetorical scheme by which to forward its identity as a progressive organization. However, in the company's promotional materials, P.O. box is listed as a "suite"—obviously an attempt to placate the more traditional potential clients who are not necessarily interested in hiring a virtual organization.

Inside an office building, the placement and type of furniture and the type, size, and location of one's office are important indicators of organizational culture and social relations. In many traditional organizations, the size of one's office and its placement operate not only as rewards for loyal or productive employees, but also serve as indications of organizational status for internal and external visitors alike. The placement and type of furniture in one's office, for example, is traditionally indicative of the organizational hierarchy, as in one organization in which employees joke about how "only those with wooden desks make decisions" (Olson, 1988a, p. 131).

An office's architectural philosophy, location, and design are most likely the decision of top executives at the highest levels of the hierarchy. However, in traditionally structured organizations, each employee is assigned an office or permanent cubicle. This area has the potential to become a personalized enclave in which employees create their own, unique individualized displays in order to share information about their extracurricular activities, political beliefs, home lives, and so forth. For instance, the posting of "Dilbert" comic strips on cubicle walls has become a genre of organizational discourse that communicates skepticism and resistance (Aden, 1998). Kunda (1992) examines the way in which individual's offices are decorated, arguing that "how members transform this standardized, impersonal space into their own territory reveals aspects of the self that they wish to convey to themselves and to others" (p. 12). The way one decorates one's desk or office not only conveys salient information to others, but also to one's self. For instance, Nippert-Eng (1996) discusses the placement of a calendar listing vacation days, softball games, and family visits on the wall of an employee's office: "Joan simply has to look up

to be reminded that, at a certain time, she'll be doing something she really enjoys, something more personally exciting
perhaps than the task at hand. The type of calendar and kind
of lettering she uses, its placement in her direct line of sight if
she lifts her head all reflect Joan's anticipation, her "looking
forward" to these events" (p. 45).

Office decoration serves a role in communicating role and
identity information to self and others, but teleworkers who
work primarily at home or in other locations do not have this
communicative avenue available to them. Although the home
offices of teleworkers observed for this study contained organizational materials such as files and other materials, they did
not typically display indicators of organizational identification
such as posters or plaques. Instead, many employees adapted
their home office environments to express their personality outside of the organizational realm. For instance, a shelving unit
holding designer dolls covered one employee's office walls; another telecommuter had a rack of guns on the wall, evidence of
a proclivity for hunting. A third telecommuter with a penchant
for fly-fishing created a little contraption, containing a minia-
ture laboratory for making fly-fishing lures (complete with mag-
nifying glass), that popped up onto his desk when he needed a
break.

Similar to the way in which technology can shape communicative patterns, geographical and architectural phenomena reflect but also can shape an organization's communicative
environment. For instance, traditional office architecture has
been replaced in many organizations by open cubicles, glass
doors, and walls that reach only halfway to the ceiling. A
Newsweek story on the "Office of the Future" described some of
these architectural innovations, claiming that "the new work
styles don't work in buildings designed for the old top-down corporation" (Hamilton, Baker, & Vlasic, 1996). The organizational
offices described in the article range from the "cave and com-
mons" design—in which employees wishing to hold a meeting roll
their desks into a common space—to buildings that include a dry
cleaner, a shoe-repair shop, and a cafeteria.

However, similar to the way in which technologically
deterministic arguments about the impacts of ICTs imbue technology itself with a kind of agency, geography alone is sometimes
credited with being the primary determinant of communication
patterns. For instance, the Newsweek article discusses the case
of one company's chief executive officer, who decided to take the
idea of cubicles a bit further:

Everyone—which includes his 65 employees and himself—sits in large cubicles that he calls "bullpens" with four other people of various ranks and functions—no walls or barriers of any kind between them. "It forces everybody to talk to each other all the time," he says. Chess says the lack of private space also limits gossip, reduces the need for memo writing, and gets top managers scattered among the troops. Every nine months or so he even stirs the pot, reshuffling everybody. (Hamilton et al., 1996)

This chief executive officer formerly worked at the White House, an environment in which employees were highly cognizant of the proximity between their offices and the president's. By creating an artificially "flat" organization through architecture and placement of desks, it is assumed that the power structure of the organization will flatten as well.

In a sense, this rhetoric mirrors the early work on CMC, which naïvely predicted that the use of CMC in organizations would result in flatter hierarchies due to the ease with which individuals could send messages directly to top management instead of having to go through filters like secretaries and lower level managers. However, while the use of CMC enables messages to be sent to anyone on the network, there is no indication that these messages will be answered or even read. Schmitz and Fulk (1991) recount an episode in which an employee attempts to use e-mail to bypass administrative layers and has the message returned along with the comment, "We don't do this around here—talk to your supervisor" (p. 515).[3]

In the same way, geography alone cannot force communicative patterns to be adopted. However, the shifting geography of work can influence the type and frequency of communication. Clearly, the sort of "bullpen" office environment described above will have a large impact on the type of communication and culture of the organization. The *Newsweek* article argues that the new office space configuration is a response to new styles of work, but through the chief executive officer's choice of the word *forces*, it is clear that this geographical structure is perceived to be more than a reflection of communicative practices that already exist. Rather it is assumed that geography has an active role in creating an environment in which talk (and change) is constant.

One question that arises from the recent shift toward the virtual or geographically dispersed organization involves the communication patterns of employees who neither congregate at a central office nor have a permanent work space. How are these communication patterns reshaped and what are the implications of this for organizational culture? In these case studies, three general patterns emerged. First, for engineers and salespeople, mobility increased as the location of work became more diffuse and dispersed. Second, the shifting geographical locus of work had the secondary effect of masking cues about the timing and duration of work for individual employees. Third, the shift prompted a shift in communication patterns within the organization, which, in some cases, resulted in changing job functions.

INCREASES IN MOBILITY

The first and primary theme that emerged from these cases speaks to the need for a reconceptualization of the notion of telecommuting. Typically presented as a home-bound housewife type in slippers and a bathrobe, today's teleworkers are in many cases actually far more mobile than suggested by previous work on the subject, which focused on the telecommunications-travel trade-offs (Nilles, Carlson, Gray, & Hanneman, 1976). This points to a need to revamp our conceptions and definitions of telework and telecommuting in order to focus on the communicative implications of this mobility.

For iLAN Systems and XYZ, ICTs were used to place people where face-to-face or hands-on contact was most valuable or necessary: with clients, for instance, or at client sites. In contrast to early work on the subject, which emphasized the way in which telecommuting could reduce travel (and therefore by-products such as automobile emissions), the teleworkers interviewed for this study were in fact *more* mobile than many traditional office workers. One iLAN engineer noted that in the past year he had put over 25,000 miles on his truck.

MASKING OF WORK-RELATED CUES

In most offices, there are cues that help workers temporally regulate their work. Formal temporal cues include the whistle for factory workers, the arrival of the next shift for waitresses, or a mandated break or quitting time recognized (and enforced) by all employees. Informal cues include the arrival or departure of other coworkers, the arrival of the lunch truck or maintenance crews coming in to empty the days' refuse, or communal lunch dates among office mates. These cues do not typically exist for teleworkers. Of course, other cues (e.g., the return of children from school) may take their place, but because these cues are not organizationally generated they may have a different degree of saliency.

Because teleworkers do not have the external cues typically provided by the office setting, they may not be able to structure their time in the same way. One iLAN engineer who had worked in a traditional office spoke about the fact that he worked longer hours at home because there was nothing to signal the end of the workday: "I remember when I used to work in an office, people started leaving, you look at your watch, okay, I'll stay a half hour more, when my boss is leaving too." This comment illustrates the subtle ways in which temporal organizational norms function. In this case, the departure of a coworker is a cue to start thinking about one's own departure.

Many employees regulate their behavior, either consciously or not, by the norms of the office. When they are removed from this environment, they typically need some time to adjust to the new patterns of the household. One XYZ salesperson spoke about how work at home had changed her relationship with her family and noted the difference between working at home and at an office:

> [It changed] at first. Because I didn't cut it off enough. Or I worked too long. Or I stopped in the evening, 5:30, 6 o'clock, got dinner going, and then went and responded to e-mail from 9:00 to 10:00 at night. And my husband does the same thing. . . . So I'm saying, we have to stop working! You have to say sometimes "My day ends at this time." You know just like if you were at the office you wouldn't stay there all night.

It would be difficult to forget to leave a traditional office; coworkers would inquire as to when you were leaving, maintenance crews would come in to clean, or other cues would indicate it was time to stop work. At home these cues don't exist.

The changing geography of work means that work and home roles need to be renegotiated—for the teleworker as well as for his or her family. As with other phenomena discussed in relation to telework, these changes were contextually affected and differed on a case-by-case basis. Some took advantage of the opportunity to work at home to shift schedules and work locations. Others (primarily salespeople and administrative people who had to interface with clients or vendors that worked traditional hours) worked fairly regimented schedules not dissimilar to those adopted by traditional office workers. Others worked a traditional 9 to 5 workday, but added extra weekend and night hours as deadlines or inclination dictated.

For example, one iLAN engineer explained that he was unfamiliar with the software package he was using, which meant that "the learning curve is quite steep. And so the only way to fix the problem is to throw more man-hours at it. . . . That means I invest more time. . . . I just add more hours."

In another case, an iLAN support person—a single, young woman—kept a traditional schedule in response to the schedules of her work associates and her peer group. Because she needed to be available to vendors during the day and her friends socialized at night, she worked a traditional 9 to 5 schedule, Monday through Friday. She explained, "In terms of my personal life, it would just fit better if I had a normal day because then that gives me the evenings to do my own personal things. And weekends . . . there are more distractions at night . . . everybody else is ready to go out at night because they've done their time."

As these comments illustrate, personal lives can add constraints as well. This teleworker's desire to maintain a traditional schedule is based on her need to socialize with her peers—which would not be possible during the day, when they are "doing their time."

CHANGES IN COMMUNICATION PATTERNS AND JOB FUNCTIONS

The shift to a dispersed work setting had an obvious impact on the communicative strategies and habits of XYZ employees, who were used to engaging in face-to-face communication with coworkers in their branch office. While iLAN Systems employees could compare iLAN to past experiences in traditional offices or talk about general differences between face-to-face and mediated communication, they did not exhibit the same feelings of loss that XYZ employees seemed to feel about their forced shift in communication patterns.

The loss of informal face-to-face communication and those aspects of organizational communication associated with it— the transmission of organizational knowledge and camaraderie—were mentioned by some XYZ employees, although others professed to be self-starters that did not need a lot of hand-holding or office chitchat. One manager observed that when employees work from home they "lose the stopping by someone's office and telling a joke, and vice versa. . . . It's just not going to happen to you. People aren't going to just call you up and tell you a joke."

For this employee, communicative behaviors that might be appropriate to enact during face-to-face communication (in this example, telling a joke) are considered somehow inappropriate for the telephone. One of the critical differences between these modes of communication is that with face-to-face communication, visual cues indicate whether someone is busy and should not be interrupted or is open to casual interaction. Unlike the telephone, this information is available before communication is initiated, through visual cues like a closed office door, or—in the case of more open office arrangements—the wearing of headphones or a certain facial expression. Some newer communication technologies allow for this information to be explicitly conveyed—for instance, most instant messaging systems allow users to indicate whether they are "available," "busy," "on the phone," and so on. In other cases, users may choose not to answer a call at certain times, though the norms governing this vary widely.

The net result, for some individuals, is that a base of informal exchange cannot be established when opportunities for face-to-face communication are limited. Therefore, when employees need information or favors from one another, there is no relationship already in place to build on. This manager uses the example of one salesperson who he rarely sees in the office:

> The only time she [comes to the office] is when she wants something from somebody, when she wants you to give something away. And there's no rapport relationship built up to try to work through something like that. There's just somebody walking through my door saying "I've got this customer and I want you to give this away." And it's like, "Well, I haven't seen you in the last six months, why should I give it away?"

This illustrates the close connections between socioemotional communication and more instrumental communication in the office. As Weick (1979) points out, seemingly pointless meetings are actually useful in that they allow participants to become familiar with one another's communicative styles. Similarly, building social capital with coworkers is instrumental and perhaps, as the above quote suggests, more challenging when face to face communication is limited.

The changing communication patterns at XYZ, in combination with the shift to the mobile worker paradigm, had the effect of changing job functions for many employees. Salespeople became less specialized and took on other responsibilities, such as doing initial pricing for orders. This was due in part to the loss of administrative staff, but also to changing communication patterns. As discussed previously, the changing geography of XYZ changed the ease with which sales engineers and salespeople could communicate with one another, therefore altering the actual content of their communication. As one sales engineer commented, "Since we've been telecommuting, the salespeople now look things up on their own before they'll call us because they can't yell over our cubicle."

This had the effect of freeing the sales engineer to "take her responsibilities a step further." However, the lessening of support staff and the redistributed geography of the organization combined to create a process by which the salespeople became "empowered"—meaning that the salespeople took on tasks previously completed by sales engineers or administrative assistants. Past research on telework has found that telework increases some individual's feelings of competency, because "they have fewer chances to ask questions of coworkers. They now try to resolve problems themselves before resorting to calling the office" (Hamilton, 1987, p. 93).

Another example of the way in which geographical changes affected communication patterns and work styles can be found in the case of a former iLAN employee, who now works full time for another organization and telecommutes from home one day a week. She took work home that required concentration home because her coworker was a "blurter":

> Donna interrupts me a lot. She's a blurter. . . . I hear her blurting all the time, and I'm dying of curiosity, so I go over there and find out what she's worried about. "What's the matter, Donna?" When I'm not there, she holds all her blurts to a couple of phone calls. And so I don't have that kind of interruption. . . . Like I hear her say "Oh no!" You know, I can't just leave an "Oh no!" hanging there. So I say "What's wrong?" over my office door. . . . If I'm not there, all of her "Oh nos," I never hear them. And if it's a really bad "Oh no" and she wants to share it with me than she'll call me. And that will interrupt [me] and we'll deal with the problem and we'll solve it. If we have to, she'll fax me something or e-mail me something
>
> INTERVIEWER: But if you're not there . . .
>
> She'll blurt her "Oh no's" out and figure out how to solve it and tell me about it later.

In this case as well, geographical separation changed communication patterns, but also behavior patterns. The coworker who can get help immediately in the office may be forced to engage her problem-solving skills when removed from this environment. This is obviously a double-edged sword, resulting in both increased confidence and increased investment of time. Removing an individual from a traditional office environment will occasion behavior changes in both this individual and those left behind at the office; both will have to be more autonomous when they encounter "Oh no's."

CULTURE: CHANGES IN MANAGEMENT AND SOCIALIZATION PATTERNS

Understanding the relationship between telework success and organizational culture is an important area of inquiry that has pragmatic implications for organizations. Future research might focus on discovering prescriptive knowledge about, for instance, which types of organizational cultures are best suited to telework. In these case studies, three themes emerged in the area of organizational culture. First, the concept of trust, contrary to some of the literature on the virtual organization, was still important and salient for both employees and their supervisors. Second, in relationships with a preexisting lack of trust, telework seemed to amplify this distrust, which led to an increase in documentation of activity and an emphasis on tangible criteria and frequent feedback. Third, teleworkers' socialization patterns changed. However, contradicting some of the research on the subject that suggests teleworkers are more isolated, many teleworkers interviewed for these case studies expressed a sense of relief at not having to socialize with coworkers as they would in a traditional office.

Before discussing the specific findings of this study, general differences between these two firms' organizational culture should be noted. The organizations differed in two important dimensions: engineer/sales relations and gender makeup. Additionally, the two organizations had different conceptions of what it meant to be "virtual." These differences may have affected the ways in which telework was adopted at each organization.

An extremely influential aspect of iLAN System's culture revolves around its status as a "virtual" company with few meetings, but many "*real* technicians doing *real* hands-on work" (Reynolds & Brusseau, 1998, p. 28, emphasis in original). XYZ adopted a mobile work model for a number of reasons, including financial concerns—but none of these factors had the same visionary appeal as iLAN's stated goal of trying to build a unique (nonmeeting) culture. It is, of course, quite possible that the rationale for initially developing iLAN without a central office was based on financial constraints, lack of real estate resources, or other less galvanizing motivators as in the case of XYZ. However, by providing the "spin" that transforms the lack of a central office from something iLAN lacks to a carefully crafted emblem of independence, the story functions to provide iLAN teleworkers with a sense of pride rather than a feeling of loss.

Another critical difference between the two organizations lies in the difference between the sales and engineering professions. Kunda (1992) and others have discussed the unique character of the engineering culture, which, it can be argued, values technical expertise over social skills. iLAN is primarily made up of engineers and has a small administrative support staff. Although XYZ and its parent company, Comco, are large multifaceted organizations that employ a variety of professionals in many fields, this study focused on the sales division of XYZ. Historically, these two professions have had a fundamentally different orientation toward technology, which may have impacted the extent to which they were able to utilize technological tools. For iLAN engineers, technology represented their livelihood as well as a source of pleasure. In contrast, XYZ salespeople typically strove for efficiency, especially in their dealings with technology. This is no doubt rooted in economics: salespeople are paid on commission, whereas technicians are rewarded for their knowledge base. In fact iLAN's Reynolds claims that if you have "a relatively inexperienced technician and he's in an area that he doesn't know about, he wants to know about it! So rather than calling a technician who does know how to do it, and finding out how to do it, he'll spend 15 minutes or 20 or an hour, 'let me try a couple more things,' 2 hours." It is in the engineers' best interest to learn new skills, which is often done by "tinkering" or trial and error. The sales staff at XYZ, on the other hand, preferred to focus on getting "face time" with clients rather than tinkering with their computers.

The difference in the gender makeup of the organizations may contribute to other differences in culture. XYZ's sales staff had roughly equal numbers of men and women, and had several women in highly technical positions and positions of power.

This is not the case at iLAN. Most of iLAN's employees are male; the women who work there are in support positions such as accounting, personnel, and marketing. Women network technicians are hard to find, and although Reynolds says he'd like to hire more women technicians, all of the technicians are male. In this aspect, iLAN is a microcosm of the larger society, in which women are less likely than men to be creators (Kramarae, 1995) or consumers of technology, as evidenced by the fact that popular culture artifacts that promote technology tend to target men (Dietrich, 1997).

So, although the predominance of male engineers at iLAN is not rare, it clearly influences the culture of the company. The metaphors and stories the organization uses to identify its purpose and its character are largely masculine: hunting, trapping, "Wild West" gunfights. These metaphors and imagery are possibly a reflection of the interests of its mostly male members, but also speak to the sense of excitement and competition that seemed to be felt by many iLAN employees. Indeed, by portraying themselves as "firefighters" of the computer world, iLAN employees proudly view themselves as performing a sort of civic duty.

Mumby (1998) argues that hegemonic processes render the role of men in the workplace invisible. Through his analysis of Kunda's (1992) *Engineering Culture*, Mumby examines the way in which masculinity is constructed among the high-tech engineers at "Tech": "For Kunda's workers, self-identity is very much tied up with work, and no such clear bifurcation of private and public selves occurs" (p. 180). This is clearly the case for iLAN engineers, many of whom cannot rely on temporal or geographical compartmentalization to bifurcate their public, work roles and their private, home roles. The employees described by Kunda (1992) worked long hours at the company office; iLAN engineers may be at home or doing errands, but they are almost always on call. For instance:

INTERVIEWER:	What's your typical schedule in terms of when you work?
ENGINEER:	There is no schedule.
INTERVIEWER:	I mean, do you work nights?
ENGINEER:	Anytime. Nights, weekends. Dave usually calls me 7:30, 8 o'clock, asking me a lot of things. Or [if he has something planned] he'lltell me that. There were times he'd even call me at 12 o'clock at night. So I mean it depends.

Many male iLAN engineers, like those described by Kunda, seemed to have a macho, almost proud, attitude about putting in long hours at work. In contrast to this open-ended work schedule, XYZ sales employees generally placed more boundaries around their work time—a process sometimes called "time-boxing"—although it was stressed that in "crunch" times, employees would often work weekends and nights.

TRUST: STILL IMPORTANT IN THE VIRTUAL ORGANIZATION

As discussed earlier, trust is commonly perceived to be a prerequisite for successful telecommuting. The literature on the virtual organization stresses the need for managers to trust their employees, since they will no longer be able to rely on line-of-sight supervision. However, these case studies contradict this simplistic notion of trust. As we know, the virtual organization carries with it many artifacts of traditional organizational structuring and, as these case studies suggest, it is *not* an entirely new organizational form unhindered by traditional organizational issues such as employee–employer trust.

The relationship between telework and trust is difficult to study. Because there is a selection bias concerning who is allowed to telework, it is hard to isolate cause and effect. In many organizations, only the most trusted, productive, or senior individuals are allowed to work off-site; therefore, it is difficult to assert that telework *causes* employees to be more trusted. However, in both of the case studies discussed here, the decision to telework was made not on an individual basis but rather was extended to all employees, which to a small degree limits this type of bias.

iLAN and XYZ took different approaches to the question of trust. At iLAN, the founders flatly denied that trust was an issue. Their approach to trust is summarized in this excerpt from a book written by one of the founders:

You're probably asking how I can trust my employees with all this responsibility and authority when I can't see them. That's an easy one. I don't trust them. I don't distrust them either. Trust is not an issue. Getting the work done is. An article appeared . . . stating that "Trust is probably the most important ingredient in a distance (telecommuting) relationship." Nonsense! What employer will defer getting productive results from a remotely located employee until some feel-good emotional bonding has been established! Not me! When I hire a technician to work from his home, I don't need to trust him, he just needs to get the job done. If he doesn't, he's toast. (Reynolds & Brusseau, 1998, pp: 30–31)

This pragmatic approach is similarly echoed in an interview with Dave Lee, the other founder:

I don't think they worry that I trust them, because otherwise they'd be out of here. It's very much black and white from that standpoint. If [your integrity] cannot be trusted, then I can't leave my place open to you over here. They have access to this place 24 hours a day, anytime they want. If they cannot be trusted for their honesty, then all my equipment could be gone. . . . Multimillion dollar equipment could be gone. So from that aspect of it, yeah. . . . I don't think that they don't believe that I don't trust them. That's the deepest level of trust. Where, in terms of the levels of trust, whether you got your work completed, that's a different level of trust. On that level, yeah, between a supervisor and a supervisee's relationship . . . you always check on them to make sure things get done. That's a different kind of trust. That one, they always say, "Dave doesn't trust us to get the things done." Okay . . . that would be the case because that's what supervisors are for, to make sure it gets done.

This second approach to trust is a bit more nuanced, but the same general underlying theme can be discerned: trust as a generalized, abstract concept is not important, but results are. If you get your work done, you will do fine at iLAN. If you do not, you will be fired. Personal or subjective feelings about an employee are not as important as objectively measured job success. Generally, employees of both firms felt trusted—as long as they were producing frequent, tangible products. For those who did not, management found other ways of monitoring work that substituted for line-of-sight management. Commonly, additional documentation detailing work processes and achievements were required; in one case, productivity reports were e-mailed on a daily basis.

When asked about the issue of trust, many iLAN employees indicated they felt trusted by their supervisors, although in a very results-based, pragmatic way. For instance, one employee said he felt trusted because he knew the founders before they started the company; another thought he was trusted because he was responsive to the founders whenever they asked him to do something. The concept of trust was usually situated within the context of productivity or, at the very least, a record of past productivity.

At both organizations, having employees off-site seemed to amplify supervisors' preexisting assessments of employee productivity. At XYZ, some managers did not agree with the decision to "virtualize" all salespeople and sales engineers. One manager explained that he felt that the decision to allow employees to telecommute should be made on a case-by-case basis. For this manager, the privilege of working unsupervised was:

> something to be earned versus something to be mandated and then I, as a manager, have to manage you [in that role]. Because it makes it more difficult. Personally, if I had to manage somebody like that, I would want them to be a very trusted person who has earned the right to work alone like that. And then, with the element of trust there, I can see their results. I don't have to constantly watch to see what they're doing. There will be other things that will indicate to me whether they're doing what's going to get the job done. And the fact of the matter is we had some people who weren't highly productive to begin with [who were] forced into going home like that. And it became— They just disappeared. They just plain disappeared.

This quote exemplifies the way in which telework amplifies preexisting dynamics, in this case centering on the issue of trust: if the supervisor already trusts the employee, he or she will assume all is well, unless something happens to indicate the contrary. As the supervisor states, "[W]ith the element of trust there, I can see their results. I don't have to constantly watch to see what they're doing." If trust is preexisting, the manager focuses on the results of the employee. However, if that trust is not there, the situation is likely to deteriorate, primarily because it will be difficult to establish trust if the employee is off-site unless he or she produces tangible results on a regular daily or weekly basis. For salespeople, who may work for months on a deal before it is solidified, this may be difficult because there are no tangible results in the interim. Ironically, employees who are not trusted might be forced to spend more time in time-consuming documentation processes to prove that they are actually working, although these activities will detract from the time they spend working.

A similar dynamic occurred at iLAN, where a situation already marked by distrust was exacerbated by the employees' off-site status. The founders were not comfortable with their ability to accurately assess the work products of two off-site employees who did not produce products the founders understood and could measure. The two employees performed job tasks that fell into a different area of functionality, and the situation was exacerbated by the geographical dispersion of the organization. Handy (1995) is often quoted for articulating the question, "How do you manage people whom you do not see?" and answering it with simple dictum, "By trusting them." An even more pressing question in this day and age might be, "How do you manage those whose jobs you do not understand?" The issue of how to supervise employees whose job functionality is not fully understood is not uncommon, especially in highly technical jobs in which output is not measurable in traditional ways.

For instance, software engineers and programmers are notoriously hard to supervise because oftentimes it is impossible to assess their work until the program is compiled and tested, sometimes months after the project was initiated. Traditional Taylorist measurement schemes in which output is measured do not work; for instance, it makes no sense to count the number of lines of code a programmer produces in a day, because often the goal is to accomplish the same functionality with fewer lines of code. Barley's (1996) study of technicians in the workplace concluded that technician's work "caused trouble for vertical forms of organizing precisely because it decoupled the authority of position from the authority of expertise" (p. 434). At iLAN, the situation is similar, only it is the manager who operates under a technical paradigm, supervising nonengineers. A combination of geographical and functional distance created a situation at iLAN in which, as one employee described it, the founders were left to ask, "What the heck is going on over there?" As discussed earlier, the supervisors then demanded more documentation from the employees, in part because they did not have a firm grasp of either the specifics of the tasks completed by the marketing staff or their significance for the company.

One of the solutions proposed in iLAN's book (Reynolds & Brusseau, 1998) on telework is the possibility of using videoconferencing to monitor employees in their homes. The authors suggest it as a transition tool for managers who may be uncomfortable with the loss of line-of-sight monitoring:

> Videoconferencing makes it easier for management to transition into the "Manage the work, not the people" mentality. I have a friend who runs an insurance brokerage. There is no reason why he needs some of his employees to come into the office. He does so for purposes of control. He recently needed one employee to make presentations in the field, alone. For the first time the boss wasn't at the presentations, and the employee wasn't in the office every day. My friend, the boss, was uncomfortable. I demonstrated videoconferencing. This was different. The boss could see if the employee was shaved, dressed and ready to work. My friend was back in control again. (p. 120)

It is unlikely that iLAN will actually implement video-conferencing for monitoring purposes, and indeed the suggestion entails ethical concerns about the use of technology for this type of surveillance. However, the concept serves as a good example of the way in which technology may be harnessed to address some of the reasons for telework's laggard adoption rate. When asked about whether videoconferencing would help allay his concerns about employees working off-site, the XYZ manager who felt telework should be a privilege reserved for only productive employees downplayed its usefulness:

> Videoconferencing isn't really going to help me because I've already established a trust relationship. I've seen what their work is, I depend on that work being done and if it's not happening [when] I know the person is capable of doing it and I've seen it in the past, I can try to address it. But if you've got someone who already has a performance problem and you send them off to work at home, they're not going to get more productive.

Again, this manager seems to suggest that trusted employees will continue to be trusted as teleworkers, whereas employees who are not productive (trusted) will become less so. This amplification dynamic is fully consistent with the social shaping perspective, which argues that technology creates opportunities and constraints, rather than predetermined effects or impacts.

FOCUS ON FREQUENT AND TANGIBLE CRITERIA

Frequency of feedback was an issue at both organizations. If the work cycle—the length of time that passed before tangible results were observed or reported—was too long, management typically wanted more documentation or direct monitoring. Salespeople are often the first to be virtualized precisely because their work products are easily monitored. However, when the time frame of a sale could be months, sales figures became less useful. As one XYZ salesperson explained, "There was one really big order that we were supposed to get that didn't come through, a really, really big order. So I'd say the first quarter has not been good for me, as it usually is. As far as the kind of things and the kind of deals I work on, I just went out and got some more. So they're in the process . . . but it's kind of like, 'What have you done for me lately?'"

In this industry, the sales performance of a slacker could look the same as one of a salesperson working successfully on a long-term, multimillion dollar contract. Similarly, at iLAN, the two employees who did not produce tangible products were asked to do daily e-mail productivity reports, quantifying their daily activities. In both organizations, "trust" was replaced with an emphasis on documentation and objective results.

CHANGES IN SOCIALIZATION PATTERNS AMONG TELEWORKERS

Research on telework shows that employee isolation is one of the primary reasons telework arrangements have not been adopted to a larger degree (Forester, 1988/1989; Olson 1988b; Pratt, 1984). In one case, teleworkers returned to the central office because they felt they had lost access to the "office grapevine" (Hamilton, 1987, p. 93). In another, "single men and women whose social life stems from office contacts" decided to stop working at home (Pratt, 1984, p. 4).

Many of the teleworkers interviewed for this study, however, seemed to replace office socializing with time spent with clients, industry contacts, or friends and family. In fact, contrary to what the literature indicates, many expressed relief at the prospect of *not* having to socialize with coworkers. As one XYZ salesperson noted, working outside a central office buffered teleworkers from office politics and gossip:

For me I'm much, *much* more productive, not only because of the distractions [at the office], but also because one of the things I don't miss is a lot of the office politics and a lot of the office gossip and quite frankly I don't miss that. Because there are always naysayers and negative people that want to meet at the coffee klatch or the coffee clutch or the water-cooler or whatever you want to call it, that now I don't have to participate in. . . . It's a big time waster. And it can put you in a bad mood.

For this teleworker, the informal communication of the office environment was associated with a loss of productivity, rather than the transmission of organizational knowledge discussed by other teleworkers. When asked about whether she missed the spontaneous exchange of organizational knowledge that typically accompanies cubicle conversations, an iLAN employee said it was "a waste of time. That's an advantage of working at home, you don't get caught up in that soap opera stuff, like a bunch of women working together and just talking all day long."

Many teleworkers interviewed for this study socialized less with office coworkers and instead focused on spending time with clients or contacts outside the organization. This shift was, in fact, one of the goals of adopting telework for both iLAN and XYZ. For XYZ, part of the goal in virtualizing the sales force was to encourage them to log more direct contact with clients and other business contacts. The justification for the eradication of permanent office space was the belief that a good salesperson is out of the office most of the time anyway—with clients, vendors, and business contacts. As one employee involved in planning the shift explained, "You've got these desks dedicated to these people and if the sales rep is doing his job he is rarely there to use that space."

In contrast, the adoption of telework at iLAN was ostensibly to avoid what the founder called a "meeting culture." When he created iLAN, according to Reynolds, he "was determined to create a culture of productivity not bogged down by needless bureaucratic or feel-good processes" (Reynolds & Brusseau, 1998, p. 27). Obviously, there were many reasons that contributed to iLAN's adoption of the telework model, and it is entirely probable that iLAN's original impetus for the lack of a central office may have been financially motivated. It is clear that to some degree, iLAN received public attention for its telecommuting efforts through an article in the *Los Ange-*

les Times and then decided to capitalize on it.[4] Regardless, the company embraced a decentralized organizational model, which clearly is well-suited to the industry iLAN is in.

In fact, even before starting iLAN, Dave Lee purportedly spent very little time in the central office, a habit he credits with his success:

> I was always wondering why people have to go to an office and then go to a customer. There's so much wasted time there, go to an office, get a cup of coffee, then talk to some people, then go to the customer. Why not just go directly to a customer? . . . People in the office, they think that they're organized, but they're a bunch of zombies holding up a cup of coffee. . . . My social network is with my customers, not in the office. I think that's where the difference is. Because if I don't have a social relationship to my customers, I don't feel right.

In both organizations, when asked about whether there was anything they did to replace "watercooler" socializing, individuals mentioned spending time with clients or associates in other companies. For instance, one iLAN support employee said:

> I'll try to make it a point to always have lunch with somebody that means potential business for our company . . . in fact I don't socialize with anyone at the office, or anyone at iLAN. . . . [A coworker] and I talk about going fly-fishing. But we never go. But I'll socialize with the clients. I've got tons of clients who like to do what I like to do. . . . Fishing. Shooting. Hunting. . . . These guys at iLAN aren't going to give me any business so why should I go out with them? [Laughter].

Others said they replaced time spent talking to coworkers with time spent talking to friends and family, the "normal people in your life." One iLAN employee complained about the ritual at many organizations of going out for drinks after work: "I always hated that because I don't want to spend my personal time with these people. I mean, I like them fine and they like me fine but I don't want to foster a relationship with them. . . . I wanted to get out of there! And they wanted me to go for drinks, and I had to go for drinks." The aspect of organizational communication that these employees resent is the loss of control associated with traditional office environments. This teleworker seems to express a sense of powerlessness about whether he socializes with his coworkers or not.

XYZ employees, however, who had experienced a traditional office environment at their company, spoke of feeling like "orphans" or "stepchildren" when they came into the office after the telecommuting initiative. They wanted to, as one salesperson said, "fully telecommute but feel like a team when [they] come into the office." This was in marked contrast to iLAN employees, who were hired with the understanding that they would be telecommuting and thus did not experience the same sense of contrast and loss.

CONCLUSION

This chapter has discussed the implications of telework at the level of the firm. Telework was socially shaped by individuals and seemed to accelerate communicative and organizational processes. It also changed patterns of management, work, and socialization. These studies reveal gaps or simplistic inaccuracies in the literature on the virtual organization and telecommuting. For instance, the issue of trust was a far more complicated issue than some of the literature indicates. The next chapter focuses on the impact of telework on the dynamics of the home and family.

Chapter Six

Telework in the Home: Calibrating the Permeability of Home/Work Boundaries

Traditionally acknowledged boundaries between the public sphere of work and the private sphere of the home are being renegotiated, as indicated by the increasing popularity of work arrangements that confuse traditional demarcations of home and work, such as telework, as well as by other cultural indicators, such as national conversations about issues of privacy.[1] The way in which boundaries between home and work are maintained by teleworkers and other mobile workers is a particularly salient research question for scholars of the social impacts of ICTs, as it provides insight into the way in which technology shapes and is shaped by interactions and individuals.

In examining the impact of telework on the home, themes relating to technology, geography, culture, and structure emerged, paralleling the changes to the organization discussed in the previous chapter. In the home arena as in the organization, these themes intertwine. Since it is impossible with this type of qualitative, contextually embedded research to isolate and test individual variables, it should be understood that although specific findings may be discussed in relation to one theme or another, this research does not intend to present findings as contextually independent events. Because of the complex nature of the interactions between technology, geography, culture, and structure, some artificial distinctions may be made for the sake of parsimony.

TECHNOLOGY: CALIBRATING THE PERMEABILITY OF WORK/HOME BOUNDARIES

Work-at-home arrangements alter traditional boundaries between public and private identities. However, the use of ICTs can potentially restructure these arenas even more dramatically. Depending on the organizational context and the way in which technologies are reshaped through individual use, ICTs can enact further blurring of "home" and "work" or they can be used to more sharply segment them. For instance, some of the respondents in this study used two telephone lines (one for business, one for personal purposes) to gain control over when and where their work identity was enacted. By changing their outgoing greeting, checking (or not checking) messages on weekends, and specially configuring the technology to suit their needs (so that a pager would go off when a voice-mail message arrived, for instance), individuals were able to regulate access to work—wherever it was physically and temporally located. Others found that having the ability to check e-mail or surf the World Wide Web while at home was a seductive pastime—sometimes to the chagrin of their spouses. Observations and interviews with teleworkers about their use of ICTs in the home revealed three dynamics or patterns of use. First, as indicated by the literature on the topic, the use of communication technologies in the home blurred boundaries between home and work for some teleworkers. Second, individuals actively used and configured ICTs to calibrate and regulate the permeability of these boundaries—the infiltration of work into their home lives and vice versa. Third, having technology in the home, especially e-mail and World Wide Web access, in concert with the lack of external cues, resulted in some teleworkers losing their sense of time, sometimes creating conflicts with family members. For these teleworkers, the availability of the World Wide Web and e-mail "beckoned" them[2]—in essence reshaping not only their work hours but also their leisure time.

ICTs AND THE BLURRING OF BOUNDARIES BETWEEN HOME AND WORK

In traditional work environments, work and home spheres are isolated geographically (and therefore, temporally, by nature of the fact that geographical travel is not instantaneous). Telework, as I have argued, eradicates geographical boundaries between these spheres. By adhering to strict schedules about when and where work takes place, however, teleworkers can re-create a sense of segmentation and distinction between their home and work lives.

For teleworkers who rely heavily on technologies such as pagers and cell phones, the ability of ICTs to reshape time complicates boundary issues. In some cases, teleworkers who use these ICTs are subject to an intense disruption of temporal boundaries, because pagers and mobile phones allow for home and work identities to be experienced simultaneously. Additionally, phone, fax, and e-mail access in the home has the potential to create a situation in which the employing organization has essentially unlimited access to the individual.

Just as the geography of an office building can influence organizational communication patterns, technology in the home affects household communication patterns. For some of the teleworkers interviewed for this study, constant and ubiquitous access to phone, fax, and e-mail technology—and therefore to work—amplified the lack of boundaries between the personal sphere and the professional sphere. Technology in the home potentially disrupts the temporal patterns of the household, because calls, e-mail, and pages from coworkers or clients can arrive at any moment, unless teleworkers have strategies in place to regulate such communication (for instance, screening calls). When these intrusions occurred, teleworkers were forced to instantly shift roles, moving from a household-identified persona to a work-identified persona. The use of ICTs made the worker, in many cases, subject to a ubiquitous form of organizational control in that they were perpetually available, accessible, and accountable.

Popular discussions of telework emphasize the liberating notion of work that can be done anywhere, at any time. It is true that telework enabled some employees to set their own schedules in which they could potentially restrict work-related activities to certain times of the day. However, when phone calls from the office or e-mail arrive at any time of the day or night, one's experience is potentially marked by a feeling of boundlessness and lack of control.

The loss of control that can accompany the use of ICTs is due to the fact that it is the presence of communications technology in the home that creates the *forced* movement from one role to another. For example, a mother may be at home eating dinner with her family when a phone call from the office forces her to adopt a work role. In this case, it is not the employee's choice to return to a work role; it is a reaction to outside events. Managers may be tacitly condoning this increased sense of boundlessness when they engage in activities such as replying to e-mail while on vacation, creating a culture in which ubiquitous access to employee time and attention is expected (Brooks, 1998). This phenomenon is not limited to teleworkers, but teleworkers who are already sensitized to the importance of maintaining visibility so as to avoid the appearance of "hiding" behind voice mail may feel more intense pressure to check and respond to messages on weekends, on vacations, and at night.

ICTs also enabled teleworkers to enact a sense of boundlessness around the geography of work when it benefited them. One teleworker, an iLAN support employee, explained, "I always have [my cell phone] with me . . . when I'm walking around the house, this is my office number. Line number one is my office, line number two is my home. So I go to the bathroom, I carry the phone into the bathroom. I go upstairs, I carry the phone with me." The organizational identity is thus diffused geographically, based on the location of the cell phone. He is able to exploit this in his dealings with clients. For instance, he speaks of one client who does not know he works from home. He tells her:

> "You're special. You have a direct line right to me!" She feels great. Fact of the matter is . . . [laughter] that's because I'm the only one here. [Laughter]. So I gave her that number! But when I'm not here I have it forwarded to my cell phone, so I don't care where I am, I will call. She always has a connection to me. The customers think that's dynamite. They've got a direct line to me. And if I'm out in my car, well, they don't know if I've left a business office or my home office.

It is critical to engage notions of access (Dutton, 1999) and the social shaping of technology perspective when exploring these issues. These technologies provide choices for individuals, but the ways in which these individuals adopt, use, and adapt these technologies are socially influenced and individually determined. Communication technologies can be liberating and constraining, sometimes simultaneously (Pool, 1990). Pagers are, for some, "an electronic leash that binds them to their jobs. Others say that the pager means freedom: No longer must they sit at their desks awaiting a call from the boss or a client" (Wilgoren, 1998). These case studies suggest that the question of whether ICTs are liberating or constraining hinges on the social and technological choices made within the home and organization, as well as the nature of one's profession.

The engineers at iLAN were particularly susceptible to disruptions to their home life at times they could not control because of the emergency-based nature of their work. For instance, the phone line set up for emergency calls to iLAN rang in the home of one of the employees. Others could be paged or called at any moment, which made it difficult to plan outings with family or friends. For instance, when asked about the drawbacks of telecommuting, one iLAN engineer replied,

> Actually the only drawback is probably my wife thinks I work too much. . . . A lot of my friends, they work in the office environment, and they don't carry pagers, they don't carry cell phones. When they leave, they leave. Okay. End of work. I carry a cell phone, I carry a pager. When I get paged, I call them back, because I don't have a choice.

As this quote illustrates, working at home and on call changes the boundaries between home and work. At the traditional office "when they leave, they leave." At home, you cannot leave work because it is always there. It is clear that telework troubles traditional geographical boundaries between home and work. But this engineer is speaking to the fact that new communication technologies intensify this attenuation of boundaries because work can no longer be *temporally* bounded either.

The nature of technical work, which is that it is extremely difficult to gauge how long any one task will take, exacerbates this lack of temporal boundaries. An iLAN engineer explained:

> [My wife will ask], "Can we do this, do that?" And, well, right now I can say "Yes" but it really depends, because if there's an emergency, I have to [work]—on weekends, sometimes . . . on weekends, mostly it's okay because our customers are off work too. But during weekdays, I can't say "Okay, let's go somewhere 5 o'clock, no problem." Or 6 o'clock, when you get off work. You know, because it really depends. And sometimes I'll tell her, "Well, I'm going to a customer now." And I can't say "Yeah, I can solve all their problems in an hour. No problem, 5 o'clock, I'll meet you." . . . I can't because [until you're there], you don't

know whether you can fix it in an hour or two. . . . There are
times when I get there, okay, 5 minutes, I'm done. There are
times we get there and then we don't leave 'til 1, 2 o'clock in
the morning.

This inability to predict or control when work takes place has the
potential to severely disrupt relationships with family and
friends. The nature of the work prevents this engineer from com-
mitting to social activities with his wife as well as to other household responsibilities. It should be noted that this phenomena is
not new—professionals such as doctors and high-level executives have traditionally been "on call" for extended periods of
time. However, compensations for these professions allow for the
use of services and goods that alleviate the strain caused by long
or unpredictable work hours—full-time nannies, for instance.

USE OF ICTS TO REGULATE INFILTRATION OF WORK INTO THE HOME

Teleworkers strategically used ICTs to manage work-related
communication while at home (Dutton, 1999). Some ICTs—for
instance, pagers—were used interchangeably for personal or
work-related purposes. Other ICTs, such as fax and phone lines,
were used more exclusively for work or were organized to provide
an element of separation between home and work. For instance,
most teleworkers had at least two phone lines, one for work-
related communication and one for personal or home use. By
choosing to answer or not answer these different lines, they
could control the influence of work into home life, and vice versa.
Sometimes teleworkers would give out their home numbers to
coworkers to use in case of emergency. However, these teleworkers typically enforced an associated set of norms regarding when
this personal number was to be used.

One XYZ salesperson spoke of her problems with one of her
coworkers, who called her personal line at times she felt were
unnecessary or inappropriate:

[One employee] was abusing my [personal] home phone
number badly, so the only ones that really have it right now
are [coworkers] Bob, Sue, and Lilly. . . . Because they only
use it in cases of emergency. . . . I just told her if she does
it again . . . I'll let all my calls at night go to the recording,
and then I'll pick them up. I mean, she was calling me . . . it
got real bad. Like, 9:30 on a Saturday night! And it's like,
"Why are you calling me?" "Well, I can't get a hold of so and

so." "Well, what am I supposed to do? I can't help you." . . .
Or she'd call me at 8 o'clock on a Sunday morning. "I need
this [price quote] redone!" Well, yeah. . . . [Laughter]. "Call
me Monday or send me an e-mail, I'm on my way out the
door to get my nails done!"

In this case, the use of two phone lines enabled this teleworker
to segment her incoming calls into work- and home-related communication. She has clear notions about which communicative
situations are acceptable transgressions and which are not, and
is able to enforce these rules by threatening to create a nonper-
meable boundary between home and work calls—by threatening
to let both lines go to voice mail and then return calls at her dis-
cretion. Although it was not available to this teleworker, technologies such as Caller ID would have assisted her in her ability
to segment professional and personal communication.

For employees who were not required to be available for
emergencies, typically administrative or salespeople, the act of
restricting access to themselves served as a ritual marking the
movement from one role to another. For instance, they would
mark the end of the workday by shutting down the computer or
forwarding their phone to voice mail. The beginning of the workday might involve changing one's voice-mail greeting and checking e-mail, as one XYZ salesperson does:

> What I do in the morning, I've got my schedule down. . . .
> I get up, I go in there [the home office], I change my voice-
> mail greeting, I log onto the network, and usually that
> time of the morning it could be a little slower than normal
> so while I'm logged on to the network no one can call me
> because it says I'm on the phone, so I jump in the shower.
> Get all that done, go downstairs, and get my tea, and by
> the time I'm done, I come up here and all my messages, all
> my [messages] are there and I can disconnect and answer
> them or whatever I need to do.

It is hypothesized that traditional office workers use their commute as an opportunity to transition from one role to another
(Salomon & Salomon, 1984). For this teleworker, the ritual of
changing her outgoing greeting and downloading her e-mail
messages is used to mark the beginning of the workday. She
has created a ritual whereby she accomplishes work-related
(downloading e-mail) and personal (showering, eating breakfast)
tasks simultaneously, symbolically mirroring the commute to

work that "simultaneously encourages us to mentally detach from and reattach to the realms and selves on either side" (Nippert-Eng, 1996, p. 119).

Teleworkers used ICTs to control when and where their organizational identities were enacted. For instance, they would develop norms around when and how often they checked e-mail and voice mail. In some cases, specific work-related communication behavior was mandated. For instance, iLAN employees were explicitly told to respond to messages within 15 minutes during working hours and within 1 hour during off hours (Reynolds & Brusseau, 1998, p. 60). This rule, which was codified after one mishap in which a key employee could not be reached because she did not have her pager with her, is one way in which the organization attempted to procedurally deal with the unique communication issues that accompany a distributed work environment.

Some teleworkers felt they had more control over their communication while working at home than they did when they worked in the office. An XYZ salesperson said,

> I get more calls done [working at home] because I don't have the interruptions—calls coming in while I'm on the phone, or someone coming up to ask me something or to get something for them. I kind of can have a little more control, I think, over my day. Because I can choose when to check up on my voice mail. I do it regularly but I don't have to stop right then because my other line is ringing.

In another case, a teleworker felt she had fewer interruptions at home, and that the interruptions she did experience at home could be more easily controlled. For instance, she had CallerID on her telephone at home and therefore could decide whether to pick up the phone once she knew who was calling. This behavior might not be considered appropriate in a traditional office environment.

Teleworkers also used communication technologies instrumentally, to manipulate their organizational identity. For example, at one point after the introduction of telecommuting, an XYZ manager broadcast a voice-mail message that ordered all employees to come into the office when not on appointments. In response, one employee who felt she was not able to do her job as well at the central office did not change her work practices, but she did change her outgoing message to indicate she was "away from her desk" rather than working from home. In this way, she was able to negotiate a solution to the conflicting desires of herself and her supervisor—in essence using the technology to create the appearance of adherence but in actuality enacting a form of resistance. In this case, the teleworker socially reshaped a technology originally intended to capture information from callers—the answering machine—and used it instead as a means by which to enact and broadcast the image desired by her supervisors. Similarly, the supervisor's use of the telephone, in which she used the broadcasting capabilities of the voice-mail system to distribute a one-directional message, was socially shaped as well.

LOSS OF SENSE OF TIME ACCOMPANYING E-MAIL AND INTERNET USE

Some employees seemed to lose track of time while working at home. This phenomenon was seemingly triggered by the eradication of external, temporal cues combined with unconstrained access to Internet technology in the home. Many teleworkers spoke of the ease with which they lost track of time while working at home on the computer. This was especially true for e-mail and Web surfing.

Telework researchers have long noted that the constant availability of the computer makes it "tempting (particularly with electronic mail) to just sign on and 'check my mail' or 'see who else is on the system'" (Olson, 1988b, p. 94). For some teleworkers, the constant availability of the computer and its related diversions meant that distinctions between work and nonwork categories became less conspicuous. As one iLAN Systems support employee explained:

> I catch myself 6:30 in the evening still on the computer doing work. Without thinking. Without noticing the time. And I catch myself at home. . . . I remember one time at two or three in the morning, I couldn't sleep, I got up, I had to get something done so I did it then. But not thinking, "Hey, that's work." And a lot of times I catch myself not wanting to watch television, and I'll go on the computer and surf the Net and find out what's going on out there in the industry. Finding out who our competitors are, finding out who else is out there that we can go to.

In this case, work-related activities replaced other traditional leisure activities, such as watching television. Some employees reported that this shift in attention caused tension with spouses. For instance, the engineer quoted previously said his wife complained that he worked too much, when he should be spending time with her. He explained, "I don't think it's 'working,' but to her it's 'working.'" The World Wide Web and e-mail are, in essence, hybrid technologies that meld business and pleasure (much like work itself), troubling dichotomies of work and nonwork. This engineer does not consider surfing the Web to be "work" but for his wife, it represents that which is not household oriented. Therefore, "to her it's 'working.'"

Another iLAN engineer explained:

> I don't mind working more hours, but I guess a lot of times [I think] "I'll do [these work-related tasks] real quick" and you end up spending more time than you actually thought you were going to, and then you have less time to do something else. At home, a lot of times I'll tell myself, it's too hot right now, I'll check my e-mail, do something, wait 'til the sun goes down, I'll wait to clean my yard. And the next thing I know it's totally dark outside! [And then I say] "Oh, well, forget it—I can't do it now!"

For this engineer, time spent checking e-mail was difficult to regulate. When he spent too much time responding to e-mail or surfing the Web, he had less time to spend on domestic or household duties, such as raking the yard. For those who work at home, having increased access to technologies like the Web and e-mail at home may result in less time spent with family, one's community, or on leisure or household activities. Depending on one's perspective, this may be perceived as encouraging tendencies of workaholism or making it possible for people to spend more time doing activities they enjoy, which also happen to be work related. One XYZ employee noted that workaholism could become a problem for some people with a tendency to overwork, but by the same token "you're not stuck in a mode where you have to get everything done between 9 and 5," which seemed to reduce stress.

The seductiveness of access at home is discussed in Reynold and Brusseau's (1998) book: "At iLAN, I have found that employees do a considerable amount of after-hours and weekend work, simply because it's so convenient for them. The computer just seems to beckon you to finish up something. Next time you turn around *it's midnight*" (p. 42, emphasis in original).

It is difficult to make claims as to whether this trend is a positive or negative development, because as with other uses of ICTs, individuals socially shape their experiences. However, it seems clear that ICTs occassioned changes in the household, creating the potential for tension and loss as well as enjoyment and satisfaction, and that over time individuals became more savvy about the complexities of negotiating household duties and paid work.

Individuals differed in the ways they organized company-related work and the extent to which they incorporated this work into their household. Some sharply segmented the two spheres. Permeable boundaries around work, either geographically, as with one teleworker who set up a desk for her children's computer next to her own, or temporally, as with another teleworker who encouraged visits from his children during the day, seemed to be the best arrangement for some. These permeable boundaries may have mitigated the problematic temporal boundlessness experienced by others, but the loss of concentration and time spent working meant hours that would have to be made up later. Csikszentmihalyi (1997) describes the loss of the sense of time as one of the characteristics of experiencing "flow." Flow is the "sense of effortless action [many people] feel in moments that stand out as the best in their lives" (p. 29). Flow is not happiness per se, although it creates feelings of happiness in retrospection. It is the sense of being completely focused on an activity to the extent that one loses track of time and effort is not self-conscious. An athlete might experience flow during a game, or a surgeon during an operation. Losing track of time while checking e-mail or surfing the Net is a widely noted phenomenon, yet it is unclear as to whether this should be considered flow. As with other themes and findings, the sense of the loss of time was not a universal component of telework for all participants. Many of the administrative people for instance, kept fairly traditional hours and did not lose themselves in work, in the way that some of the engineers did.

GEOGRAPHY: NEGOTIATING THE DEMANDS AND CONSTRAINTS OF SPACE

In the home, telework impacted the geography—and therefore the politics—of the household in three distinct ways. First, working at home occasioned renegotiations of space in the household. These negotiations were often embedded in the political and social context of the home. Second, for some teleworkers, especially women, working at home had a unique set of distractions from those experienced at "the office." Third, it was sometimes difficult for teleworkers to separate work and home spheres of their identity, because the traditional geographic distinction between personal and professional roles was not present when they worked from home.

For these individuals, the introduction of paid work into the domestic sphere brought with it many attendant changes. Geographical changes—mainly, the need to create an office in the household—were for some the earliest and most concrete indication of how all-encompassing these changes would be. The circumstances surrounding the creation of the home office and the ways in which teleworkers carved out work space were indicative of underlying household tensions and priorities. For instance, an office created in a space that had been used for domestic purposes—the room of a child away at college—might indicate the changing focus of a parent with older children.

In addition to disrupting existing patterns of household communication and geography, bringing work into the home had the potential to cause conflicts and financial strains. In one case, a young, single woman with a roommate had to move into a larger apartment in order to create an office area that did not intrude on communal space. In another case, a teleworker and her husband went to a marriage counselor to resolve conflicts over office space in the house. The XYZ salesperson had turned a room that was previously used by a live-in nanny into her office but had difficulty communicating her needs for privacy and exclusivity to her husband:

> I turned that room into an office because I was telecommuting out here. . . . And, um, he didn't regard that as my office. He thought it was part of his house, [so] it was his office and he could go in there anytime he wanted. And it was an issue for us because I said, "Hey, wait a minute! That's my office, my work space. Do you go into someone else's office at work and sit at their desk and use their phone? And move their stuff?" . . . He didn't see it as my work space. So, the marriage counselor helped him see that and he realized that.

This type of negotiation about work space was not atypical, although this was one of the more extreme cases. In this case, the couple tried various work arrangements unsuccessfully before settling on an arrangement where the husband would bring a laptop and other equipment to the dining room table and would work there during his occasional work-at-home days.

Other teleworkers shared offices, with varying degrees of success. In one case, a family in which one parent worked from home every day and the other only once a week created an office that could be reshaped as attention or eardrums demanded. The husband had a small office attached to a small room that housed computers for his wife and child. When the husband got too "animated" on the telephone, she would shut the door. Otherwise, as she said, "Usually just the sound of his voice doesn't bother me."

In another case, an iLAN support employee, the oldest son of an Asian family, chose to have his office in the front room of his mother's home. This worked out well for both himself and his mother. An elderly woman, she was not able to drive and wanted to move to a more urban area where it would be easier for her to get to the doctor's office and grocery store. The teleworker, fearing for her safety, offered to move his home office into her front room and drive her when she needed to do errands or visit the doctor. Because he can drop her off and then arrange to pick her up later, his schedule is not significantly affected. As he explained, "This was actually the perfect setup for her and for me since I'm the oldest in the family and probably the only family member close enough around 'cause I live just maybe a couple of miles away. We thought it'd be best for me to set up the office here and take care of her needs when they came up." In this case, telework enabled this individual to fulfill what he may have perceived as familial obligation while also completing his organizational duties. The occasional trips to local stores did not significantly affect the amount of time he spent working but made a substantive difference in his mother's quality of life.

Being able to shut the door, literally, on work made it easier for teleworkers to balance the work and home components of their identities. A married couple that both worked from home spoke of their previous house, which did not have an extra bedroom that could be used as an office. This was problematic because they had their work materials in the living room, and often one or the other would have a work-related thought in the midst of relaxing or watching television, would then go to write it down, and would become engrossed in work. They found this disruptive because they preferred to carve out time, especially in the evening, when they could wind down, eat dinner, and have "personal time" with each other. Because they both worked at home for the same organization, this was important. When they moved to another house with an extra room they converted into an office, they found it much easier to confine work to a specific location within the home, which made it easier for them to create temporal boundaries around work as well.

Interviews with teleworkers revealed that the home and the office each had a distinct set of distractions. The office environment had "blurters," gossip, and office noises, whereas the home had intrusions from spouses, pets, children, and telemarketers. When asked about the drawbacks of working at home, one female former iLAN employee said:

> The drawbacks are characterized by that cartoon right there [she points to a cartoon taped on the wall]. It's basically having to have the mental focus to take my eyes off everything in the house. . . . The drawback [of working at home] is you have to discipline yourself to ignore the pile of stuff you left undone in the bedroom that you really wanted to get to when it's time to get to work. When you're at the office, you can't do anything about it and it's totally away from you. . . . I'm a crafts kind of a person, I like to do projects. [When I'm working at home,] sometimes those things . . . *call* me to them.

Familial transportation responsibilities constituted another claim on teleworkers' time. Many participants, especially those with children living at home, took breaks from work to drive family members to work or to school or to do errands. Depending on the frequency and duration of these intrusions, teleworkers made up the missed time later in the day. As a general rule, teleworkers did not complain about distractions like these and in some cases valued the opportunity afforded by transportation chores to interact with their children.

Other teleworkers found it difficult to work at home while domestic duties were left undone. Interestingly, one woman believed that the ability to mentally parse out household demands from work demands was gender related. Her husband (an iLAN employee), she said, was not as distracted by household chores or craft opportunities: "He's not as distracted by household stuff. I think it's a guy thing . . . I call it the 'gift of invisibility.' For men it's a gift, that stuff is invisible. He doesn't even see it." This was echoed by another female teleworker, who found it hard to work if the house was "messy" or "cluttered." In fact, during a joint interview, when a male teleworker was asked whether it bothered him if the house was messy when it was time to work, his wife quickly answered for him: "No, it doesn't bother him. It bothers me."

Teleworkers often created physical separations between work and home spaces, mirroring the traditional geographical separation of the two. Having an office with a door that closed was desirable, because it could be used to indicate to the teleworker and his or her family whether interruptions would be welcome. One XYZ salesperson said she did not think that working at home blurred the boundaries between her professional and her personal life because, as she explained, "it's not an issue for me. I mean I know the difference. . . . Plus I have an office—I go into the office and work."

In other cases, employees created symbolic distinctions between home and work roles. One couple, Pete and Linda, who both worked at home for iLAN, developed a way to communicatively re-create the CLOSED sign hung on stores and businesses:

LINDA: [S]ometimes when he's in [the home office] at 8 o'clock, I'm screaming at him, "iLAN is closed!" That's what we say, usually when it's time . . . "iLAN is closed."

PETE: Yeah, at the end of the day: "iLAN is closed!"

LINDA: And then we don't talk about work anymore.

The irony of this, of course, is that iLAN never closes. The presence of the organization is constant. However, by closing the door to the office and telling each other that "iLAN is closed!" the two are able to carve out a time and place for their home lives. Others have noted the tendency to communicatively construct boundaries that are traditionally represented by places or objects; for instance, Kunda (1992) writes that employees will "indicate one's presence at the non-existent [office] door by saying knock-knock" (p. 193).

CULTURE: CREATING NEW RULES AND NEW COMMUNICATION PATTERNS

Households differed in how telework was shaped within the home and the ways in which ICTs were used to make boundaries more or less permeable. Teleworkers and their families created new rules, new communication patterns, and new ways to enact boundaries between home and work in response to telework. Employees and their families were creative in constructing boundaries and in using communication technologies to manage these boundaries.

NEW RULES AND BOUNDARIES

Families adjusted to telework by creating and enforcing norms surrounding work. Some families encouraged children's participation in their work life by allowing geographical proximity between personal and professional spaces or by letting the children help with aspects of their job. Others enforced a strict separation between the two. In cases where work occurred in one geographic area of the house, a specific code of conduct was often enforced. One teleworker, for example, said his kids knew not to come into his office unless they "smelled smoke or saw blood." Children were instructed about communicative and behavioral norms surrounding work. As one teleworker said, "Even my son—he'll come in the room [but will] write a note if he needs something or try not to disturb my phone call." In this case, family members recognized the office as a place where work happens and communication must be controlled.

Other teleworkers preferred to incorporate their family into their work space, in ways that did not affect their productivity but made them feel connected to their family and household, as one XYZ support employee relates:

> In my particular case, I have taken a desk that's in our family library—the desk is something I used to use to write the household checks and do household work—and I have literally moved anything related to the home out of this desk. So now my office is literally a 3-feet × 3-feet square. A desk and a chair. . . . Actually come to think of it I kind of share a little space with my kids because I've got my rolltop desk and I've got my laptop on it and right next to it is a computer I've given to my kids for their video games and they can do their homework on it. A lot of times in the afternoon one of my children will come in and will actually work at that computer and will do their homework or put headphones on and play a video game right next to me. They don't talk to me at all, but we're right next to each other and they don't feel alone and neither do I.

In this case, although the teleworker and her children do not explicitly communicate with one another, personal and professional spaces are successfully incorporated.

New patterns of communication emerged in many households, but families with more than one person working at home seemed to find telework more challenging than households with only one teleworker. In one household in which husband and wife both worked for the same company, the couple exhibited frustration over the constraints placed on their conversation style by their tightly coupled work relationship. In response to a question about the most significant drawback of working at home, the wife said, "Not being able to say, 'How was your day, dear?'" Her husband added with a moan of frustration, "We can't! I don't want to hear how her day was and she doesn't want to hear how mine was, because we live this together. She knows how my day was! *Argh*!"

NEW USES OF COMMUNICATION TECHNOLOGIES

Employees and families showed creativity and resolve in constructing boundaries from available materials and in using communication technologies to fortify or whittle away boundaries when needed. For instance, one teleworker explained how his mind would often be "somewhere else" while at home. When asked about cues the teleworker might use to indicate to his family that he was working, he answered, "[M]y eyes will not be looking at them [laugh]—[or I will] just not answer [them], or just stay in my room." This employee's family eventually learned to call him on the business phone line in his office to get his attention. As he explains it, "They could come and talk to me, [but] I don't hear them. They call me on the business phone, I'm going to answer."

In this situation, by not communicating with his family, the employee has limited their access to him while he is working. However, because he is attentive to the telephone line that is supposed to be dedicated to work-related communication, his family strategically uses it to regain his attention. This is an apt example of the way in which ICTs do not cause specific actions to occur but rather reshape access (Dutton, 1999). In this case, the employee has reshaped access to himself by attending only to work-related messages, and his family has creatively exploited this communication channel in a creative work-around designed to get his attention.

STRUCTURE: BRINGING WORK INTO
THE HOUSEHOLD

The structure of the household encompasses and influences many of the phenomena previously discussed in relation to telework and the changing technology, geography, and culture of the household. The structure of the household in this case refers to the size and elements of the household as well as its underlying power dynamics. For instance, a young single woman living with a roommate has a very different household structure than does an older man living with his wife and three children, and this will influence the way in which telework and ICTs are used and socially shaped in each environment.

In many ways, the structure of the household is just as important as the geographical constraints discussed earlier. In many of these cases, geographical barriers had to be shifted in order to make room for work-related furniture and materials, but how this was done ultimately depended on the structure of the household. For instance, one teleworker, living with his wife and three teenaged children, encountered some difficulties in making room for an office in his full household. He had an office in his son's bedroom until he moved out to the family's attached garage, where he shared space with the laundry facilities. During an interview that took place in his living room, the iLAN employee pointed to one of the walls and explained:

> I was on the other side of this partition here which was a dining room; I put that wall in there. Unfortunately, my son shared one end of it and I was at the other. We had a little curtain there and we had no privacy and it was just not comfortable . . . he didn't have any privacy and I didn't have much privacy and so we had a family meeting and my daughter says well, you have to move out into the garage. [Laughs]. I said, "Okay."

Later in the interview, a disembodied voice that seemed to be emanating from the wall corrected one of his answers. It was apparent that the separation between the two rooms—a thin layer of plasterboard that conducted most of the sound between the two rooms—was inadequate for a home office. His garage office was more private but so small one could sit in the center and touch all four walls with only slight stretching.

Geographical and financial constraints differed among the teleworkers involved in this study, depending on the structure of the family and the size of the residence, but teleworkers showed creativity in finding solutions. In one case, a young single woman changed apartments in order to comfortably work at home. In another case, a husband and wife sought marriage counseling to help them work through some of the territory issues that accompanied the introduction of work into the household.

Working at home also meant that the structure and therefore the politics of the household infiltrated the politics of work, especially when more than one family member worked for the same organization. When a high-ranking iLAN employee hired a family member who had previously lived with his family, the power structure of the household provided a template for the organizational power structure. The employee explains:

> [The employee/family member] was living with us since . . . college. She graduated from college and . . . over the years, I had no trouble telling her what to do—"If you don't do it then I [will] just get rid of you and [then you won't] have [to] do it anymore"—over the years different things I asked her to do around the house. So in terms of the chain of authority, it's never been a problem.

In this case, the organizational structure and the structure of the household reinforced one another. The patriarch of the household also had a position of power within the organization, and these powerful roles reinforced one another in the household.

In another case, telecommuting enabled a female iLAN support employee to be more receptive to the needs of her family. She explained: "[When I work at home,] when they want something, or they want something cooked, I can cook it for them. If they want something, they can get it, most of the time right away. They like that. At work, they call me and say 'Mom, I want this.' I say, 'What can I do? I'm at work.'" In many cases the gender makeup of the household impacted the way in which the challenges posed by telework were managed. In this case, the family adopted telework in such a way that the teleworkers' domestic responsibilities increased when she worked at home, because she was more accessible to her family and their demands. Other families might shape telework differently. It might be used to lesson the teleworker's household responsibilities, for instance. In another household, the husband, who worked at home, refused to do certain household chores but instead paid for a cleaning woman.

This chapter has discussed the ways in which telework impacted the household and the ways in which individuals and their families used information and communication technologies to calibrate the permeability of their home/work boundaries. The introduction of paid work into the private sphere of the home affected individuals in unique ways, suggesting that technology, geography, culture, and structure are critical factors to consider when examining telework.

Chapter Seven
Moving Forward in Telework Research and Practice

Through an embedded case study of two organizations, this book has explored the ways in which individuals use ICTs to socially shape their home and work environments and to negotiate the many changes that accompany the introduction of professional concerns into the domestic sphere. Teleworkers and their supervisors used ICTs to try to ameliorate many of the problems noted by telework researchers—for instance, the difficulties of knowledge transfer among employees who are not co-located, the challenges of shifting from a "supervision-by-observation" to a "supervision-by-results" paradigm, and the frustrations inherent in accessing specific information (both digital and analog) when and where it is needed. In the home, teleworkers used ICTs as a tool for calibrating the permeability of their home/work boundaries. A pragmatic implication of these case studies speaks to the critical nature of adequate technical support and network access for mobile workers.

As this study has illustrated, the social shaping lens is useful for understanding these behaviors in that it acknowledges the ways in which ICTs foreclose or create possibilities rather than "cause" impacts or effects. Technologies such as e-mail, cellular phones, and database technology seem to amplify and reinforce existing trends or tendencies surrounding the separation of home and work boundaries as well as other issues faced by teleworkers. These case studies illustrate some of the opportunities, constraints, and changes afforded by ICTs, and no doubt more will emerge as we increasingly rely on technology-mediated communication to conduct our work and social lives. As we move from traditional bureaucracies to more fluid and less hierarchical forms of organizing, questions of how to share knowledge in a dispersed organization, how colleagues will create and maintain social connections, and the changing nature of work itself will continue to emerge. This book hopefully offers some insights into these processes, but much more work is needed before we can confidently construct theoretical models that address the multiple social aspects of technological change in the household, organization and society.

ICTs in the Home and Workplace

As ICTs allow us to further rearrange time and space, the geographical dispersion of the firm will continue to trouble traditional models of organizational structure and management. For instance, we know that observation-based supervisory mechanisms are flawed, yet many find the thought of abandoning them altogether to be threatening. Moving employees out of the central office is uncomfortable for traditional managers, but this discomfort is magnified exponentially by the fact that the nature of work itself is changing. In other words, shifts in the "where" of work are made more complex by accompanying shifts in the "how" and "what" of technology-related jobs such as computer engineering.

Today's managers are not only struggling to manage those they cannot see, but also to manage those whose work products they do not understand, or those whose work products are so tightly coupled with nonwork products that attempting to distinguish between the two is futile. Managers in the past probably found it easy to discriminate between work and nonwork activities. Gossiping at the coffee pot might have been cause for chastisement 30 years ago, but today many organizations create lounges specifically to encourage cross-disciplinary fertilization and culture building. In the past, reading the newspaper at the office may have been seen as unprofessional, but today many professions entail surfing the Net to gather research and news. As managerial paradigms continue to shift and organizations become more mobile, telework may come to represent not so much a drastic change in practice but rather another variation on the larger theme involving the geographical and temporal diffusion of work.

The social arena is experiencing technological and social change as well. More households are getting connected to the

Internet via broadband connections (Nielsen/NetRatings, 2003) and some children are growing up in a media environment in which cell phones, instant messaging, and MUDs (multi-user dimensions) are ubiquitous. As one college student says, real life "is just one more window, and it's not usually my best one" (cited in Turkle, 1995). ICTs like cell phones are spawning new patterns of communication, for instance, "swarming," in which packs of young people coordinate face-to-face meetings instantly and nonhierarchically by forwarding text or voice messages (Garreau, 2002; see also Rheingold, 2002). Communication within the household now includes children instant messaging their peers from the computers in their bedrooms, parents checking work-related e-mail on weekends, and Grandma using videoconferencing to check up on the new baby. As the domestic sphere becomes more saturated with media and communication opportunities, our conceptualizations of public and private spaces will continue to evolve. Although some strong work has been done in the area, there exists a continuing need for theoretical models and frameworks that address the changes that accompany our increasing use of ICTs and our adoption of nontraditional organizational arrangements such as telework.

TELEWORK: THE AMPLIFICATION THESIS

The changes that accompanied the adoption of telework at iLAN Systems and XYZ varied in significant ways—telework, like technology in general, does not have predetermined or predictable effects on communication patterns, organizational processes, or culture. These examples suggest that telework reinforced and accelerated existing organizational processes and social dynamics. For example, a situation that was marked by distrust became more so with the addition of geographical distance. Similarly, a family that enjoyed positive relations with one another seemed to thrive when one parent worked from home, and individuals who were truly excited by their profession used the increased access to work provided by telework as a means by which they might spend more time doing an activity they enjoyed.

This dynamic of acceleration or amplification has been noted in several other arenas unrelated to telework, such as organizational structuring (Barley, 1986) and interpersonal communication (Wilcot, 1995). In the interpersonal realm, this dynamic is similar to communication spirals, which occur when the actions or behavior of one individual in a relationship magnifies the actions or behavior of the other (Wilcot, 1995). Danziger, Dutton, Kling, & Kraemer (1982) observe a parallel dynamic in the political sphere and suggest that the reinforcement politics perspective offers the best explanation of why computerized information systems had different political effects when installed in cities dominated by various parties. The reinforcement politics perspective, which can be considered under the rubric of social shaping approaches, "predicts that computer-based systems tend to follow and reinforce the existing pattern of power relationships" (Danziger, Dutton, Kling, & Kraemer, 1982, p. 187).

In fact, early commentaries on telecommuting perceived a similar dynamic in terms of the relationship between telecommuting and marital stability. As a 1986 book on telecommuting implementation noted, "It's a good bet that telecommuting can make strong marriages better, may push weak ones over the edge, and make those in the middle get better or worse quite quickly" (Gordon & Kelly, 1986, p. 108). In some respects this observation is true for organizations as well. Adoption of a dispersed work force has the potential to make strong organizations better but may "push weak ones over the edge." This interpretation of telework as an accelerating and enhancing force fits squarely with the social shaping perspective in that it acknowledges that the impacts of a technology such as telework are not wholly dependent on either the technology itself or the social environment. Rather, the adoption of telework is a dynamic and social process. My use of the term *social shaping* implies an active process in which participants have agency but technology creates opportunities for change. This perspective, which draws attention to the fact that telework amplifies certain aspects of organizational and household life, offers a direction in which to focus future telework research and a means by which to reinterpret past findings.

Telework arrangements typically involve more mediated and less face-to-face communication. Sometimes this communication takes place among organizational members who have prior knowledge and experience with one another, sometimes not. As scholars have noted, e-mail and other forms of text-based communication do not include nonverbal communication, such as tone of voice, gestures, body language, and pauses in speaking. This has resulted in the characterization of CMC as a "thin" medium (Daft & Lengel, 1986; Trevino, Daft, & Lengel, 1990). Nonverbal communication cues, which traditionally convey nuances associated with tone of voice and expression (such as irony and humor) have been replaced with emoticons such as "smiley faces," which are utilized by CMC participants in informal fora to address this gap and provide vital contextual information (Baym, 1995). However, current organizational communication norms do not allow for the inclusion of emoticons in organizational or business-related written communication. It is possible that normative restrictions on the use of emoticons in business communication have the effect of limiting a common practice by which users contextualize their electronic communication. As business norms surrounding the use of CMC continue to evolve, other compensatory practices introduced into the business communication repertoire will no doubt enable CMC to be a more powerful conduit of informal and emotionally nuanced communication in the organizational arena.

GEOGRAPHICAL AND SPATIAL ASPECTS OF TELEWORK

Telework entails a renegotiation of space because work is no longer restricted to just the traditional workplace, typically the centralized office. This renegotiation involves changing patterns of communication and socialization, work practices, and temporal boundaries in both the organizational and the household arenas. For engineers and salespeople, mobility increased as the location of work became more diffuse and dispersed—contradicting popular depictions of home-bound telecommuters. Second, the shifting geographical locus of work masked external temporal cues, which made it challenging for teleworkers and their families to create and adhere to constraints around when and where work was enacted. Third, the shift to telework prompted a shift in communication patterns within the organization, which had the secondary effect of changing job functions.

In the home, telework impacted the politics and the geography of the household in three distinct ways. First, working at home occasioned renegotiations of space in the household. These renegotiations were often embedded in the political and social context of the household. Second, for some teleworkers, especially women, working at home had a unique set of distractions stemming from the household. Third, working at home complicated the process of psychologically separating one's personal and professional spheres.

At both iLAN Systems and XYZ, telework and the use of ICTs enabled these organizations to place people where face to face communication or physical placement was most valuable and/or necessary. In contrast to popular conceptions of home-bound telecommuters conducting audio conferences while dressed in pajamas and slippers, many of the teleworkers involved with this study were very mobile and worked from many locations, not just their home offices. For instance, one of iLAN's founders reported that he spent 70 percent of his time at customer locations and only 30 percent at his home or the Help Desk. This mobility was enabled by the use of ICTs such as pagers, cell phones, and faxes. These technologies reshaped the geography of work so that it was no longer necessary to go to a centralized office in which employees were co-located in order to access information, communicate with coworkers, and engage in other work-related practices. ICTs enabled teleworkers to do these things from their homes, client sites, or from iLAN's Help Desk or XYZ's telecommuting cubicles, allowing them to strategically concentrate their use of face-to-face communication. Face-to-face communication was reserved for situations in which physical presence was either necessary or desirous.

The increased mobility of teleworkers in these cases represents a challenge to the way telecommuting is represented and conceptualized in popular depictions as well as academic study. It is important that telecommuting research that focuses on the trade-offs between telecommunications and transportation (e.g., Nilles, Carlson, Gray, & Hanneman, 1976) continue, because of the crucial environmental issues it addresses, but this study suggests that the more interesting aspects of telecommuting from a social science perspective are masked by this focus on travel. The notion of telecommuting aptly describes a substitution of one locale (i.e., the home) for another (the centralized workplace). The term *telework* can help direct attention to the fact that work is occurring outside of traditional place-based limitations. This realization may complicate popular notions of geographically constrained home-based workers and, hence, broaden the discussion to engage other salient issues such as the role of ICTs in reshaping work. Reconceptualizing and broadening the notion of telework will enable social science researchers to engage in grounded, context-based work that engages a wide spectrum of concerns in many areas, such as psychology, sociology, and communications, rather than focusing on only travel-related issues.

Goddard and Richardson (1996) make the astute observation that, contrary to popular arguments that ICTs will make geography obsolete, technology in fact can *enhance* geographical characteristics and allow organizations to more fully exploit geographical differences: "The successful implementation of telematics widens the 'locational repertoires' available to organizations. This does not mean that geography in the sense of differences between places no longer matters. . . . [T]elematics enables organizations to exploit very small differences between locations" (p. 200). In the cases described in this book, these "small differences" are things such as an added hour of productivity previously spent commuting to an office and, more importantly, an emphasis on linking employees to specific locales only when necessary. This may be, in the case of iLAN, when engineers need to reinstall a computer server at a customer's building or, in the case of XYZ, during a client meeting. The reshaping of geography enabled by telework was purposely crafted by both organizations to limit face-to-face communication to situations in which it was necessary or valuable.

As spatial barriers become less important, organizations become more sensitive to variations of place (Goddard & Richardson, 1996). Individual teleworkers, too, became more attentive to place issues once their traditional relationship to the geography of the office was challenged and reshaped. For instance, the Irvine employees who were moved to Anaheim were highly cognizant of what they saw as the less-than-professional trappings of the Anaheim office. For some, it seemed as if the worn carpet and furniture reflected the company's attitude toward the salespeople. This difference may have been magnified by the contrast to home offices, as illustrated by one employee's reaction to the Anaheim cubicles: "I'm going to come in here? And work in this mess? When I've got a really great office at home that's fully operational? I don't think so!"

Geographical and cultural factors are intertwined in any organization, but telework emphasizes and complicates the nature of the connection. Teleworkers who may have taken face-to-face communication with coworkers for granted are made more aware of the intimate linkage between proximity and important, albeit sometimes invisible, communication practices, such as informal sharing of organizational knowledge. It is, as one participant explained, harder to "learn from what others are winning from" when employees are not co-located. Although organizational culture is not limited to the geographical arena of the office and it is possible for informal communication to be shared via ICTs, many employees may find this transition difficult. For some, the use of ICTs for informal communication feels unsafe, as illustrated by the fact that some salespeople were uncomfortable entering sensitive data into a database and preferred to communicate the information via telephone. For others, the use of ICTs for informal communication feels artificial: as one participant explained, "People aren't going to just call you up and tell you a joke."

Popular conceptions of the virtual organization link physical and structural decentralization—in many cases it is assumed that physical decentralization will inevitably lead to other types of decentralization. The use of cubicles as opposed to traditional offices is expected to promote a more egalitarian work environment, for instance. The social shaping perspective and these case studies suggest that geography, like technology, can create opportunities for change. How these opportunities are enacted depends on underlying social factors. So, the geographical dispersion of an organization will not explicitly or predictably result in decentralization, an increase in trust, or empowerment of employees. If the cultural bias of management is to hoard power or to monitor employees, ICTs can be used for surveillance purposes (e.g., through the use of digital video cameras, as *Cyberlane Commuter* suggests) or to limit the access of employees to information.

TECHNOLOGICAL ASPECTS OF TELEWORK

Technology—specifically, the use of ICTs by teleworkers—impacted the way in which telework was socially shaped in the home and the way in which work was structurally shaped in the organization. In the home, the use of communication technologies blurred boundaries between home and work for some teleworkers, although individuals actively used and configured communication technologies to calibrate the permeability of their work and home roles. Having technology in the home, especially e-mail and World Wide Web access, in tandem with the lack of external cues, resulted in a loss of the sense of time for some teleworkers, sometimes creating conflicts with family members.

Several aspects of these cases point to the tightly coupled and recursive relationship of structure and technology, which has been discussed in other contexts (Barley, 1986; Orlikowski, 1992). For instance, the use of ICTs enabled quick and decentralized communication among iLAN's engineers—they were able to directly contact one another when needed, rather than submit queries to a department manager. ICTs were also used to eradicate traditional boundaries around where and when work occurred: note the iLAN founder's penchant for calling engineers at night, from his cell phone, as he drove home from seeing a client. In another example, the family members that called their father or husband on his work line used ICTs to make the home/work boundaries enacted by the teleworker more permeable than perhaps he would have liked. His attempts to ignore physical (household-related) cues while in his home office were sabotaged by his family, who used the work telephone line to masquerade as work-related communication.

These case studies also illustrate the ways in which organizational culture shapes the use of ICTs. In situations marked by employee/employer distrust, ICTs were used to control work or to substitute for direct managerial monitoring, such as in the case of the iLAN employees who had to produce daily e-mail productivity reports. In another case, the new president of XYZ used a videoconference to "meet" the sales staff at various locations and deliver her introductory speech. Although she encouraged questions and input from her audience, the process was very much a "one-to-many" form of communication, reinforcing the culture and hierarchical structure of the firm.

THE CULTURE OF TELEWORK

Themes, belief systems, and shared assumptions can be located across organizations, but each organizational culture is unique, dynamic, and continually re-created by individuals (Martin, Feldman, Hatch, & Sitkin, 1983). For this and other reasons, it is difficult to generalize about the interaction of telework and organizational culture. Each telework situation is influenced by many factors, including organizational norms, the type of work being done, and the set of skills and constraints that determine whether each teleworker is working at home out of choice or necessity (Olson, 1987, 1988b). So, for example, Salomon and Salomon (1984) look at the social role of the workplace and note that it is different for "low level workers" than it is for managers and professionals.

Also, work will have different degrees of salience and meaning for individual teleworkers, given the broad range of occupations suitable for telework (Wright & Oldford, 1993). Therefore, this study's observations about teleworkers are not intended as generalizations about all organizational cultures and telework or as statements about how telework will impact individuals, families, or household units across economic strata, type of work, organization, and family unit. Rather, this study should be read as an exploration of two unique organizations and the way in which these cultures adapted to the changes introduced by telework.

In these case studies, three themes emerged in the area of organizational culture. First, the issue of trust, contrary to some of the work on the virtual organization, was still an important and salient issue for both employees and their supervisors. Second, in many cases, particularly when there was a lack of trust, telework led to an increase in the required documentation of activity and an emphasis on tangible criteria and frequent feedback. Third, teleworkers' socialization patterns changed. In the home, telework was socially shaped by the culture of the household. Teleworkers and their families created new rules, new patterns of communication, and new, creative uses of communication technologies.

The intimate and recursive relationship between structure and culture is best exemplified by the lack of support and resources for telecommuting at XYZ after the departure of the president, who had been a key proponent of telecommuting. This was for reasons that were both cultural, in that the project was slightly stigmatized because it was associated with an individual that had left the company, as well as structural, in that few had the authority to delegate financial resources to the initiative. At iLAN, the lack of meetings can be seen as a function of both cultural norms (influenced by the founders' philosophical aversion for them) and structural, in that the flatness of the iLAN hierarchy and the relative independence of the engineers made meetings less necessary.

FUTURE DIRECTIONS FOR TELEWORK RESEARCH

In addition to the themes of technology, geography, culture, and structure emerging from this study, a review of the literature on telework suggests several areas for future research. I suggest that telework researchers continue to pay attention to the role of technology, conduct more longitudinal and context-sensitive research, make more attempts at synthesizing past research and literature, and examine more fully the reasons why telework arrangements are discontinued.

The role of technology in enabling telework and possibly mitigating some of the key barriers to its adoption is an important area to explore. Technological advances over the past decade have had a significant impact on the daily experiences of many mobile workers. However, it is not uncommon for researchers to fail to distinguish between early research (from the 1970s and early 1980s) on teleworkers and more recent work, although the communicative environment has shifted dramatically. Researchers looking at issues such as isolation should acknowledge the differences between today's teleworkers, who have access to mobile phones, e-mail, fax machines, the World Wide Web, and pagers, and the experiences of earlier teleworkers. More work should be done to understand the ways in which communication technology tools might ameliorate or intensify some of the social and psychological problems experienced by teleworkers.

More longitudinal research needs to be done to gain a greater understanding of possible honeymoon effects, noted by researchers in regard to both satisfaction with telework (Forester, 1988/1989; Huws, Korte, & Robinson, 1990) and the relationship between managers and telecommuters (Reinsch, 1997). As Kraut, Steinfield, Chan, Butler, and Hoag (1998) point out, longitudinal research would help determine whether communication technologies are able to *create* organizational identification or merely support or maintain it.

Additionally, as discussed earlier, it is important that telework researchers conduct contextually embedded telework research. It is clear from these studies that the social impacts of telework cannot be assessed or understood independently of the underlying contextual environment. Context-sensitive research might also resolve some of the conflicting findings of the extant telework research.

I also suggest researchers make more attempts to synthesize past research and literature. This research should consider all levels of impact, rather than focusing on one. Belanger and Collins (1998) write that "it is important to conceptualize and measure outcome criteria separately, since in any distributed work arrangement, outcomes for individuals, organizations, and society may be contradictory" (p. 146). They note that, for example, telecommuting might have positive implications for the organization but negative ones for particular employees. Since these variables interact with one another, researchers should develop models that can take each of these levels into consideration and explicitly acknowledge the relationship between individuals, households, and organizations.

Finally, more research should examine the failures of telework, not just the success stories. For instance, Chiat-Day was an early proponent of the distributed organization, but moved away from this model after discovering employees were storing office files in their trunks. The lessons learned by telework practitioners should be incorporated into academic examinations of telework. Specifically, understanding the reasons some companies move away from teleworking experiments will be useful for designing future distributed work arrangements.

CONCLUSION

This study uses grounded, reality-based case studies of two organizations to study the impacts of telework on the organization and the household. Themes of technology, geography, culture, and structure were suggested by these cases and were used to guide discussion and analysis. These cases revealed that telework in many ways reinforced underlying tensions and tendencies. Most important, these cases suggest that telework is socially shaped, both in the household and the organization. This study cannot—nor was it intended to—address all the questions surrounding this complex topic. Indeed, it is hoped that aspects of this book will raise more questions than it answers, for both researchers and practitioners of telework.

Appendix

A Note on Method

This study utilizes an embedded case study design, in which "within a single case, attention is also given to a subunit or subunits" (Yin, 1984, p. 44). Three levels are considered: the two organizations, the branches or units within each organization, and the individual teleworker. Because the impacts of telework are felt at the level of the organization and the household, individual teleworkers are considered within both contexts. Although other studies of organizations and technology have surveyed employees from different organizational contexts, in this case it was critical that individual interviews be considered in conjunction with the organizational context.[1] Research on computer-mediated communication should consider appropriate and multiple levels of analysis (Rice, 1992). Because the focus of this study is the impact of telework on individuals in both the organization and the household, it is important to consider the organizational, domestic, and individual variables in relation to one another.

This study was conducted as an embedded case study utilizing interview and observation techniques, although within the course of the project, adjustments were made in order to more accurately describe and understand the effects of telework. These small adjustments stemmed from the fact that the design of the study was open enough to consider new developments while maintaining methodological rigor:

Unless the [research design of a case study] is very general, it is usually transcended, supplemented, or left behind as the developing field work suggests new topics and hypotheses. It is important, therefore, that the design be loose enough to allow for developments in the field; too strict a design ties the research down and inhibits the changes in concepts that are characteristic of field work. (Diesing, 1971, p. 143)

THE IMPORTANCE OF CONTEXT

The organizational context is vital to consider when examining the questions with which this study is concerned. As Fulk, Schmitz, and Schwarz (1992) note, models that focus on social context effects have become more prevalent. This has occurred partly in response to the limited ability of technologically deterministic approaches to explain technology use in organizations, as indicated by conflicting evidence found in studies testing media richness theory (Schmitz & Fulk, 1991). Although survey data can be used to assess the impact of telework on specific factors (e.g., employees' feelings about their productivity), other aspects of telework are difficult to assess via this methodology. Survey methodology, used in many technology and organizational communication studies, cannot accurately and completely capture the contextual details that may come into play in specific telework situations. As Fulk and colleagues (1992) argue:

> For researchers to ignore the historical context when investigating CMC is to risk excluding critical variables, treating complex and dynamic processes as static and misspecifying as local in origin those imperatives over the shared beliefs and behaviors that groups enact as part of a distinctive "culture." And the decontextualization that this entails may create not only frustration in attempting to draw valid conclusions across sets of conflicting findings, but also missed opportunities for developing context-specific theories of the contexts of computer-mediated communication in organizations. (p. 18)

Consideration of context may serve to resolve some of the apparent contradictions in previous telework research.[2] Contradictory findings found in some organizational literature, such as those considering the effects of technology on organizational structure (Barley, 1986),[3] can also be found in research on telework. For instance, research on the effects of telework on family life has been inconclusive (Hill, Hawkins, & Miller, 1996) and it is unclear as to whether telework arrangements decrease or increase identification with the firm (Bailyn, 1989; Olson & Primps, 1990; Wiesenfeld, Raghuram, & Garud, 1998). Some of these inconsistencies may be due to preexisting contextual differences, such as organizational culture variables that existed prior to the introduction of telework.

Contextual information is often left uncovered by surveys. Because telework may accelerate or acerbate underlying processes in organizations, contradictory evidence about the impact of telework should be treated, as Barley (1986) argues in another context, as a "replicated finding" (p. 78), not the product of methodological or theoretical flaws. He writes: "One suspects that traditional cross-sectional studies that see large sample size and ignore contextually embedded dynamics would risk concluding that scanners have no implications for the social organization of radiology because differences in formal structures would tend to cancel each other in correlational analysis" (p. 105–106). Barley's observation holds true for studies examining the impact of telework as well. Issuing a survey to a large number of respondents at various organizations would most likely find change on a number of telework-related variables. However, these findings when analyzed in a vacuum of contextual information could be interpreted incorrectly. Additionally, as Barley points out, in cases in which a variable fluctuates in opposite directions in two or more organizations, these changes would cancel each other out rather than alert researchers to the different processes taking place at various sites.

XYZ AND iLAN SYSTEMS:
A TALE OF TWO ORGANIZATIONS

After learning of XYZ's plans to virtualize its employees and move the office to another location, researchers visited the Culver City branch office in late 1996. On-site observation and several interviews were conducted, focusing on various aspects of the shift to mobile work. Contact with the organization was reestablished by the author in early 1998. Participants for the study were identified by the vice president of human resources or through a snowball sampling method, in which employees suggested other participants. The second organization in this study, iLAN Systems, was also included as a case study in an earlier research report and was contacted for this project. An initial meeting was set up with Tom Reynolds at his home office and other iLAN employees were contacted either through Reynolds or the voice-mail system or were encountered at the Help Desk.

Interviews typically lasted between one and one and one-half hours, although some were much shorter, particularly with the few individuals who did not telework. The longest interview lasted four and one-half hours. Interviews were recorded using a small recorder and were transcribed by the researcher. When possible, interviews were conducted in individuals' homes, although some interviews, especially early ones, were conducted by telephone and recorded or were conducted face-to-face at the Help Desk (iLAN) or the Anaheim office (XYZ). Interviews conducted in homes of teleworkers often resulted in serendipitously encountered information and a far greater sensitivity on the part of the researcher to the issues involved in bringing work into the home. For example, participants offered tours of their home offices and equipment, demonstrated their technological "toys" (such as videoconferencing), and generally seemed more likely to share personal details and observations.

Interviews focused on issues that stemmed from a review of the telework literature as well as related topics (e.g., home/work balance).[4] The interview protocol included questions focusing on individuals' roles and duties within both the organization and the household, as well as questions concerning the use of ICTs in both arenas. Demographic information was also gathered.

Questions addressed telework at the level of the organization and household. Questions regarding the organization focused on job duties, management issues, and use of ICTs. Questions designed to tap into the social aspects of the workplace were included as well. These questions regarding the home arena focused on the potential for blurring of home and work roles as well as changing family relations and the temporal aspects of working at home.

At iLAN, both founders were interviewed extensively. Additionally, the wife and son of one of the founders were interviewed, as were most of the technicians and all of the support staff. Fifteen iLAN participants were interviewed in all. Some participants, such as the founder Tom Reynolds, were interviewed or contacted on numerous occasions.

At XYZ, 12 participants were interviewed, which included several levels of management as well as sales engineers and account managers. XYZ was a particularly challenging case due to the geographical dispersion and high turnover rates of the organization. Additionally, salespeople who worked on commission were less likely to donate time, which might otherwise be spent making sales. Several XYZ participants were reapproached on several occasions via phone calls and e-mail in order to keep abreast of organizational changes over time.

LIMITATIONS

This study should not be, nor was it intended to be, used to make generalizations about the larger population of teleworkers. Instead, the study was designed to be a contextually sensitive investigation of two organizations and the ways in which telework affected the organizations, their individual employees, and these employees' families and home lives. It is hoped that the themes uncovered by these interviews and analysis are useful for guiding future research. Additionally, this project aimed to explore the ways in which the social shaping perspective would prove useful in understanding these phenomena. Additionally, without longitudinal research, it is unclear which of the phenomena studied were related specifically to telework. For instance, during the course of the study, XYZ experienced a large reorganization, layoffs, and the absence of key executives. These events probably affected employees in myriad ways, which cannot be discovered without additional, detailed longitudinal research.

Notes

CHAPTER 1. THE SOCIAL AND ORGANIZATIONAL DIMENSIONS OF TELEWORK

1. As the workday in one country ends, some global teams hand off files to colleagues in another part of the world, effectively creating a work cycle that is 24, rather than 8 to 10, hours in length.

2. The ideal type of virtual organization is envisioned as having the following features: (1) the replacement of material files with electronic, flexible files; (2) the replacement of face-to-face with computer-mediated communication for the purpose of transferring information and conducting business (with an increase in the role of face-to-face communication for maintaining organizational identity); (3) a shift in organizational structure, in which the structure itself is less visible and more flexible; (4) an increase in networking among organizations and a blurring of interorganizational boundaries; and (5) the implosion of bureaucratic specialization into cross-functional computer-mediated jobs (Nohria & Berkley, 1994).

3. As summarized by a 1998 popular press article, "while the booming economy and new technologies mean that work is spilling into the homes of millions of Americans, personal pursuits are also creeping in[to] the office. . . . Viewed this Labor Day from either direction, the lines between work and home are blurring" (Wilgoren, 1998).

4. This study is also apropos given the increasing trend toward small organizational pods in which one or sometimes two employees conduct business within another larger organizational environment, presumably complicating their feelings of identification. For instance, small kiosks in shopping malls often house one employee, who is not proximate

to any coworkers, and banks now place one employee and a laptop computer in grocery stores.

5. Predictions about the impacts of technology seem to resurface cyclically. For example, Pool (1990) quotes Marshall McLuhan on the impact of the telephone: "The pyramidal structure . . . cannot withstand the speed of the telephone to bypass all hierarchical arrangements. . . . Today the junior executive can get on a first name basis with seniors in different parts of the country" (p. 69). Interestingly, the filtering mechanism that is currently associated with voice mail and receptionists is precisely the phenomenon that e-mail was to make obsolete, just as the telephone was predicted to "bypass all hierarchical arrangements" (p. 69).

6. For instance, the electric rather than the gas refrigerator was adopted not because it was better designed but rather because it was backed by a large organization with more money for publicity (Cowan, 1985). Other research in this vein looks at the domestication of technologies (Silverstone, 1994, 1996) and the political realm (Danziger, Dutton, Kling, & Kraemer, 1982).

7. Orlikowski's (1992) structurational model of technology has three components: human elements (designers, users, and decision makers), technology (the material artifacts mediating task execution in the workplace), and institutional properties of organizations (the business strategies, culture, control mechanisms, expertise, communication patterns, government regulation, etc.). The model assumes that institutional properties influence human agents, which influence and are influenced by technology, which then influences institutions.

8. Barley's (1986) study of the impact of CT scanners on the organizational structure of work found that the same technology occasioned different structural outcomes. He examined the introduction of identical technology (CT scanners) into two hospitals, which resulted in divergent forms of organizing and different structural outcomes. The scanners became "social objects whose meanings were defined by the context of their use" (p. 106)—resulting in one hospital becoming structurally more decentralized. This research argues that the role of technology is to trigger, which leads to social dynamics that have unintended structuring consequences. Technology triggered change in departmental structure by altering institutionalized roles and patterns of interaction.

9. At the request of the company, the name of the organization has been changed.

10. *Cybercommuters* is a term iLAN uses in its book on the subject of telecommuting. It describes a remote worker who "lives and works on the Web, using and sharing cyberdata, communicating with cyberprocesses and collaborating with cybercolleagues with cybertools" (Reynolds & Brusseau, 1998, p. 150).

CHAPTER 2. WHAT WE KNOW
ABOUT TELEWORK

1. For instance, Olson and Primps (1984/1990) define telecommuting as "the substitution of telecommunications for physical travel to work" (p. 189) and when the Department of Employment in the United Kingdom conducted a large survey of firms using teleworkers, the use of technology figured prominently in two of the five criteria (Parliamentrary Office of Science and Technology, 1995). However, Mokhtarian (1991a) includes in her definition of telecommuting remote supervision and reduced commute travel—but not necessarily telecommunications technology.

2. Work in this area often attempts to gauge the effect of telecommuting on urban geography and planning. For example, Nilles (1991) examines the impact of telecommuting on urban sprawl; Sato and Spinks (1998) discuss the transportation consequences of a Tokyo earthquake; and Goldman and Goldman (1998) examine the adoption of telework from a policy perspective. Mokhtarian and her colleagues have published extensively on the transportation implications of telework; see Mokhtarian (1991b) for a review of the literature on the subject.

3. Even telecommuting practioners do not agree on the numbers: the president of the American Telecommuting Association has stated that his group considers the numbers overstated, whereas the executive director of TAC/International Telework Association believes the numbers may be understated (Wells, 1997).

4. A detailed report of factors influencing the adoption of telecommuting in Southern California can be found in Park, Nilles, and Baer (1996); also see PS Enterprises (1995).

5. The boundaryless organization is defined as an organizational form with "flatter hierarchies, . . . flexible, reconfigurable information infrastructures" (Mankin, Cohen, & Bikson, 1996, p. 241). This vision of the virtual or boundaryless organization is more rhetorical than actual. While many organizations display certain characteristics of the virtual organization, a very small number exist as purely "virtual." Indeed, the virtual organization may be more usefully conceptualized as a spectrum or "matter of degree," rather than a specific type of organization (Kraut, Steinfield, Chan, Butler, & Hoag, 1998).

6. Work may also be more secure than the home: Hochschild (1997) points out that in her study one participant had worked for the same company for 30 years but had remarried twice and lived with or dated several other women. She writes, "Increasing numbers of people are getting their 'pink slips' at home. Work may become their rock" (p. 45).

7. One telecommuter could not concentrate while at home because his dog, who was used to his master playing with him when at home, barked too much (Wells, 1997).

8. A *New Yorker* article titled "Dial-a-Wife" details another solution: hiring someone to do the domestic duties "wives used to do before so many of them went to work" (Talbot, 1997, p. 196). An alternative solution is utilized by management theorist Charles Handy and his wife: for one half of the year, he takes on no outside engagements and takes care of the house and his wife's photographic career; during the rest of the year, his wife manages the household and handles professional arrangements for him (Lyall, 1997).

9. There are some indications that men are spending more time on household duties and child care, and that women are spending less (Robinson & Godbey, 1997). This trend may carry over into households with women teleworkers.

Chapter 3. iLAN Systems: A Distributed Work Environment from Inception

1. Other than Tom Reynolds, whose identity would be impossible to securely conceal, all names here have been changed to protect participants' anonymity.

2. As is the case throughout this book, these observations were true at the time of data collection, but may be different today.

3. Firms often utilize contract labor because this allows them to quickly adjust staffing levels, but these part-time employees typically do not receive the same benefits as full-time employees. In fact, many activists fear that firms will use telework as a way to transform full-time jobs with benefits into contract positions, which receive no benefits and lower salaries (Christensen, 1987, 1988a).

4. In the book chapter on the subject, titled "Support and the Lost Soul," Reynolds recounts how his wife's employers expect her to maintain her home computer. If her computer malfunctioned (and iLAN did not exist), she would have to look through the yellow pages to find a support shop and bring the machine to them on her own time. The shop, according to Reynolds, has a 1 percent chance of being able to solve the problem correctly with no loss of data.

5. The "sniffer" is a diagnostic tool used by network technicians that provides information about a computer network (i.e., how efficient it is).

Chapter 4. XYZ: Remote Management's Commitment to Telework

1. Data were collected between 1996 (directly after the announced relocation of the Culver City, California, office) and 1998

(when the company welcomed a new president). Therefore, this description should be viewed as a snapshot of one period in this organization's history rather than a document reflecting the current state of affairs at XYZ. Also, the name of the organization and all individuals have been changed to protect participants' anonymity.

2. Response levels were so low that the survey is not useful for the purposes of statistical analysis, but the open-ended responses by two employees and one manager shed some light on their experiences and feelings about the organization and its transition to telecommuting.

3. SmartFocus conducted these surveys for the purpose of gathering information about the new organizational structure and the extent to which various positions could or should be virtualized. Results of the surveys, while useful as organizational artifacts, should not be treated as valid or unpolluted data for several reasons. There is the clear danger of bias both on the part of the administrators of the survey and the respondents. There are also indications that some respondents were concerned that the information "might be used against them" and therefore manipulated their responses in such a way to emphasize or de-emphasize their ability to work without a permanent office. Additionally, both surveys had very low response rates. The extremely small number of respondents in each position and the reportage of the results made confidentiality of respondents highly suspect, and in some cases it would be a simple task to match responses to their originators.

4. Two of these speeches were made in a large room of Anaheim employees from all departments, and a third was conducted via videoconference with sales staff in the region.

CHAPTER 5. TELEWORK AND THE ORGANIZATION: CHANGING PATTERNS OF MANAGEMENT, WORK, AND SOCIALIZATION

1. Current debates about the Open Source software movement speak to this notion—compare the underlying philosophical orientation of Microsoft products, in which the code is hidden, inaccessible, and opaque, to Linux, a free Unix-based operating system. Linux's source code is freely available to all and users are encouraged to contribute to it.

2. For instance, see Barley's (1983/1991) examination of the furnishings of a funeral home and Van Maanen's (1991) discussion of Disneyland as the "Smile Factory" in which the theme park setting is a vital component of the analysis. Kunda (1992) describes an organization's office building as reflecting the "openness" and "flexibility" prescribed by its culture (p. 46).

3. Another example of this can be found in the political sphere. Communication technology enables e-mail messages to be sent to the president via an e-mail link on the White House Web site, but only the most naïve citizen would believe his or her message was actually received by the president.

4. This is made clear in Reynolds's comments about iLAN's telecommuting initiative:

> What are we doing it for? We're doing it because it's a feeder. We make our money just like most companies at the high end of the business, designing and troubleshooting large networks. Telecommuting to us is not a business. . . . We're not *in* the telecommuting business. We're not selling telecommuting, frankly. What we're using [is] basically what [the *Los Angeles Times* writer] and you and [another researcher] and everybody else did, to basically define us as the telecommuting experts. Thanks very much. . . . [W]e're using it [as a marketing tool] to get our name out. We're experts now in something! That's why I spent all the energy to write a book! Not because I care about writing a book, well . . . but now we're established as experts. That's a hot topic. Now we're experts in something. People we talk to—we talk to people—our plan is to talk to 100 people a week in . . . 20 minutes [at] these Rotary club seminars. But from a marketing point of view, that's an awful lot of people whose business cards you pick up and you send a letter to and literature to, and it's a prospecting process.

CHAPTER 6. TELEWORK IN THE HOME: CALIBRATING THE PERMEABILITY OF HOME/WORK BOUNDARIES

1. One such conversation is the 1998 debate surrounding the controversial Starr Report, which raised issues over the private space of the presidency. In President Bill Clinton's August 17, 1998, televised speech to the American public, he said, "Now, this matter is between me, the two people I love most—my wife and our daughter—and our God," and told the audience that "it's nobody's business but ours. Even presidents have private lives." Through his insistence that the matter was "nobody's business," Clinton incorporated the widely held belief that the home constitutes a private, almost sacrosanct, arena, not open to public debate or censor—though he himself is a public figure. The juxtaposition of public and private in this story culminated in the

release on the Internet—arguably the most public of media—of Kenneth Starr's report detailing intimate aspects of the president's personal life.

2. As explained in *Cyberlane Commuter*, "At iLAN, I have found that employees do a considerable amount of after-hours and week-end work, simply because it's so convenient for them. The computer just seems to beckon you to finish up something. Next time you turn around *it's midnight*" (Reynolds & Brusseau, 1998, p. 42, emphasis in original).

APPENDIX. A NOTE ON METHOD

1. For instance, Rice (1993) used survey data from six organizations (from various studies published from 1987 to 1993), to compare media use. This type of approach would be entirely inappropriate for this type of study because organizational culture variations would be lost.

2. In other cases, even aspects of telework that are generally undisputed are revealed to be inadequately measured and poorly defined (Belanger & Collins, 1998).

3. Barley (1986) points out that "as most investigators admit, after two and a half decades of research our evidence for technology's influence on organizational structure is, at best, confusing and contradictory" (p. 78).

4. Some early interviews included a question about whether working at home had affected participant's involvement with the community, but this question was dropped when it became apparent that individuals reported either no change or change based on the increased amount of time they spent at local restaurants.

References

Abreu, S. (2000, June 19). How to manage telecommuters. CNN.comRetrieved January 19, 2003, from http://www.cnn. com/2000/TECH/computing/06/19/telecommuting.idg/

Aden, R. (1998). *Exiled in Cubeville, striving for Nerdvana: Dilbert as a critique of phony meritocracy.* Paper presented at the annual convention of the Western States Communication Association, Denver, CO.

Ahrentzen, S. (1990). Managing conflict by managing boundaries: How professional homeworkers cope with multiple roles at home. *Environment and Behavior, 22*(6), 723–752.

Armour, S. (1998, January 29). Working at home raises job site safety issues. *USA Today,* p. B1.

Baig, E. (1998, October 12). Saying adios to the office. *Business Week.* Retrieved February 9, 2003, from http://www.businessweek. com/1998/41/b3599149.htm

Bailyn, L. (1989). Towards the perfect workplace? *Communications of the ACM, 32*(4), 460–471.

Barley, S. R. (1986). Technology as an occasion for structuring: Evidence from observations of CT scanners and the social order of radiology departments. *Administrative Science Quarterly, 31,* 78–108.

Barley, S. R. (1991). Semiotics and the study of occupational and organizational culture. In P. Frost, L. Moore, M. L. Louis, C. Lundberg, & J. Martin (Eds.), *Reframing organizational culture.* Beverly Hills, CA: Sage. (Originally published in *Administrative Science Quarterly, 23,* 393–413, 1983)

Barley, S. R. (1996). Technicians in the workplace: Ethnographic evidence for bringing work into organization studies. *Administrative Science Quarterly, 41,* 404–441.

Baym, N. K. (1995). The emergence of community in computer-mediated communication. In S. Jones (Ed.), *Cybersociety: Computer-mediated communication and community* (pp. 138–163). Thousand Oaks, CA: Sage.

Beach, B. (1989). *Integrating work and family life: The home-working family.* Albany: State University of New York Press.

Belanger, F., & Collins, R. W. (1998). Distributed work arrangements: A research framework. *The Information Society, 14,* 137–152.

Bell, D. (1973). *The coming of post-industrial society: A venture in social forecasting,* New York: Basic Books.

Berger, W. (1999, February). Lost in space. *Wired, 7.02.* Retrieved December 15, 2002, from http://www.wired.com/wired/archive/7.02/chiat.html

Bijker, W., & Law, J. (Eds.). (1992). *Shaping technology/Building society: Studies in socio-technical change.* Cambridge, MA: MIT Press.

Braverman, H. (1985). Technology and capitalist control. In D. MacKenzie & J. Wajcman (Eds.), *The social shaping of technology: How the refrigerator got its hum* (pp. 81–83). Philadelphia: Milton Keynes and Open University Press.

Brodsly, D. (1981). *L.A. freeway: An appreciative essay.* Berkeley: University of California Press.

Brooks, N. B. (1998, December 6). For some, technology just makes work obligations ever-present. *Los Angeles Times,* p. C5.

Brown, J. S., & Duguid, P. (2000). *The social life of information.* Boston: Harvard Business School Press.

Chesbrough, H. W., & Teece, D. J. (1996, January–February). When is virtual virtuous? Organizing for innovation. *Harvard Business Review, 73*(3), 65–73.

Christensen, K. (1988a). A hard day's work in the electronic cottage. In T. Forester (Ed.), *Computers in society.* Guilford, CT: Duskin. (Reprinted from *Across the board,* pp. 17–21, April 1987)

Christensen, K. (1988b). Introduction: White-collar home-based work—The changing U.S. economy and family. In K. Christensen (Ed.), *The new era of home-based work: Directions and policies* (pp. 1–11). Boulder, CO: Westview Press.

Contractor, N., & Eisenberg, E. (1990). Communication networks and new media in organizations. In J. Fulk & C. Steinfield (Eds.), *Organizations and communication technology* (pp. 143–172). Newbury Park, CA: Sage.

Costello, C. (1988). A case study of work and family. In K. Christensen (Ed.), *The new era of home-based work: Directions and policies* (pp. 135–145). Boulder, CO: Westview Press.

Cowan, R. S. (1985). How the refrigerator got its hum. In D. MacKenzie & J. Wajcman (Eds.), *The social shaping of technology: How the refrigerator got its hum* (pp. 53–54). Philadelphia: Milton Keynes and Open University Press.

Cross, T. B., & Raizman, M. (1986). *Telecommuting: The future technology of work.* Homewood, IL: Dow Jones–Irwin.

Csikszentmihalyi, M. (1990). *Flow: The psychology of everyday experience.* New York: HarperPerennial.

Daft, R., & Lengel, R. (1986). Organizational information requirements, media richness and structural design. *Management Science, 32*(5), 554–571.

Danziger, J. N., Dutton, W. H., Kling, R., & Kraemer, K. L. (1982). *Computers and politics: High technology in American local governments.* New York: Columbia University Press.

Davidow, W. H., & Malone, M. S. (1992). *The virtual corporation.* New York: Harper Business.

Davies, R. (n.d.). Telecommuting: Culture, social roles, and managing telecommuters. Conference Proceedings: Telecommuting and Employee Effectiveness. Retrieved March 10, 1999, from http://www.mcb.co.uk/literati/articles/telecom.htm

Davis, D. D., & Polonko, K. A. (2001, October). *Telework in the United States: Telework America Survey 2001 executive summary.* Retrieved February 15, 2003, from http://www.working fromanywhere.org/telework/twa2001.htm

Dickerson, M. (1998a, October 7). Women are geared for growth. *Los Angeles Times,* pp. C1, C10.

Dickerson, M. (1998b, November 4). For "Mamapreneurs," industry begins at home. *Los Angeles Times,* pp. C1, C8.

Diesing, P. (1971). *Patterns of discovery in the social sciences.* Chicago: Aldine Atherton.

Dietrich, D. (1997). (Re)-fashioning the techno-erotic woman: Gender and textuality in the cybercultural matrix. In S. Jones (Ed.), *Virtual culture: Identity and communication in cyberspace* (pp. 169–184). Thousand Oaks, CA: Sage.

Di Martino, V., & Wirth, L. (1990). Telework: A new way of working and living. *International Labour Review, 129,* 529–554.

Dutton, J., Dukerich, J., & Harquail, C. (1994). Organizational images and member identification. *Administrative Science Quarterly, 39,* 239–263.

Dutton, W. (1996, August 31). *The virtual organization: Tele-access in business and industry.* Report prepared for the Fujitsu Research Institute, Tokyo, Japan.

Dutton, W. (1999). *Society on the line: Information politics in the digital age.* Oxford, UK: Oxford University Press.

Duxbury, L., Higgins, C., & Mills, S. (1992). After-hours telecommuting and work-family conflict: A comparative analysis. *Information Systems Research, 3*(2), 173–190.

Duxbury, L., Higgins, C., & Neufeld, D. (1998). Telework and the balance between work and family: Is telework part of the problem or part of the solution? In M. Igbaria & M. Tan (Eds.), *The virtual workplace* (pp. 218–255). Hershey, PA: Idea Group.

Eisenberg, E., & Riley, P. (2001). Organizational culture. In F. M. Jablin & L. L. Putnam (Eds.), *The new handbook of organizational communication: Advances in theory, research, and methods* (pp. 291–322). Thousand Oaks, CA: Sage.

European Commission. (2000, September). E-work: Status report on new ways to work in the information society. Retrieved January 18, 2003, from http://www.eto.org.uk/twork/tw00/pdf/tw2000.pdf

Evans, A. (1993). Working at home: A new career dimension. *International Journal of Career Management, 5*(2). Retrieved May 4, 1997, from http://www.mcb.co.uk/services/conferen/hrn/icem/reading2.htm

Fishman, C. (1996, August). We've seen the future of work. *Fast Company.* Retrieved February 9, 2003, from http://www.fastcompany.com/online/04/work.html

Forester, T. (1989). The myth of the electronic cottage. In T. Forester (Ed.), *Computers in the human context.* Cambridge, MA: MIT Press. (Reprinted from *Futures, 20*(3), June 1988)

Fritz, M., Higa, K., & Narasimhan, S. (1995). Toward a telework taxonomy and test for suitability: A synthesis of the literature. *Group Decision and Negotiation, 4,* 311–334.

Fulk, J., Schmitz, J., & Schwarz, D. (1992). The dynamics of context-behavior interactions in computer-mediated communication. In M. Lea (Ed.), *Contexts of computer-mediated communication* (pp. 7–29). London: Harvester-Wheatsheaf.

Fulk, J., Schmitz, J., & Steinfield, C. (1990). A social influence model of technology use. In J. Fulk & C. Steinfield (Eds.), *Organizations and communication technology.* Newbury Park, CA: Sage.

Fulk, J., & Steinfield, C. (Eds.). (1990). *Organizations and communication technology.* Newbury Park, CA: Sage.

Garreau, J. (2002, July 31). Cell biology: Like the bee, this evolving species buzzes and swarms. *The Washington Post,* p. C1. Retrieved August 12, 2002, from http://www.washingtonpost.com/wp-dyn/articles/A23395-2002Jul30.html

Giddens, A. (1984). *The constitution of society: Outline of the theory of structuration.* Berkeley: University of California Press.

Gilhooly, K. (2001, June 25). The staff that never sleeps. *Computerworld.* Retrieved July 14, 2002, from http://www.computerworld.com/careertopics/careers/training/story/0,10801,61588,00.html

Ginsberg, S. (1997, April 27). For some workers, going it alone is a cool thing to do. *The Washington Post,* p. H4.

Gladwell, M. (2002, March 25). The social life of paper: Looking for method in the mess. *The New Yorker,* pp. 92–96.

Goddard, J., & Richardson, R. (1996). Why geography will still matter: What jobs go where? In W. Dutton (Ed.), *Information and communication technologies: Visions and realities* (pp. 196–214). Oxford, UK: Oxford University Press.

Goldman, L., & Goldman, B. (1998). Planning for telework. In P. Jackson & J. van der Wielen (Eds.), *Teleworking: International perspectives from telecommuting to the virtual organisation* (pp. 207-214). London: Routledge.

Gordon, G., & Kelly, M. (1986). *Telecommuting: How to make it work for you and your company.* Englewood Cliffs, NJ: Prentice-Hall.

Gordon, G. E. (1988). The dilemmas of telework: Technology vs. tradition. In W. B. Korte, S. Robinson, & W. J. Steinle (Eds.) *Telework: Present situation and future development of a new form of work organisation* (pp. 113–136). Amsterdam: Elsevier Science.

Grimsley, K. D. (1998, November 27). Company towns are back and booming: Changing labor market turns employers into landlords. *The Washington Post,* pp. A1, A24–25.

Guthrie, R. D. (1997). The ethics of telework. *Information Systems Management, 14*(4), 29–32.

Haddon, L., & Silverstone, R. (1995). Telework and the changing relation of home and work. In N. Heap, R. Thomas, G. Einon, R. Mason, & H. Mackay (Eds.), *Information technology and society: A reader* (pp. 400–412). London: Sage.

Halal, W. E. (1996, November). The rise of the knowledge entrepreneur. *Futurist, 30*(6), 13–16. Retrieved from Journal Express database (UMI).

Hall, D. (1990). Telecommuting and the management of work–home boundaries. *Paradigms revised: The annual review of communications and society* (pp. 177–208). Nashville, TN: Northern Telecom Inc. and Queenstown, MD: Aspen Institute.

Hall, D., & Richter, J. (1988). Balancing work life and home life: What can organizations do to help? *Academy of Management Executive, 8*(3), 213–223.

Hamilton, C. A. (1987, April). Telecommuting. *Personnel Journal,* 91–101.

Hamilton, J. O., Baker, S., & Vlasic, B. (1996, April 19). The new workplace: Walls are falling as the "office of the future" finally takes shape. *Newsweek,* 106–117. Retrieved February 8, 2003, from http://www.businessweek.com/1996/18/b34731.htm

Handy, C. (1995). Trust and the virtual organization. *Harvard Business Review, 73*(3), 40–50.

Handy, C. (1996). *Beyond certainty: The changing world of organizations.* Boston: Harvard Business School Press.

Harpaz, I. (2002). Advantages and disadvantages of telecommuting for the individual, organization, and society. *Work Study, 51*(2), 74–80.

Harrington, S. J., & Ruppel, C. P. (1999). Telecommuting: A test of trust, competing values, and relative advantage. *IEEE Transactions on Professional Communication, 42,* 223–239.

Hill, E. J., Hawkins, A., & Miller, B. (1996). Work and family in the virtual office: Perceived influences of mobile telework. *Family Relations, 45*(3), 293–301. Retrieved September 6, 1998, from Journal Express-UMI.

Hill, J. (1995). The perceived influence of mobile telework on aspects of work life and family life: An exploratory study. *Dissertation Abstracts International, 56,* 10A.

Hochschild, A. (1997). *The time bind: When work becomes home and home becomes work.* New York: Metropolitan Books.

Holderness, M. (1995, February 3). Caught in the Net. *New Statesman and Society, 8*(338), 31–32.

Huws, U., Korte, W., & Robinson, S. (1990). *Telework: Towards the elusive office.* Chichester, UK: Wiley.

Hylmö, A., & Buzzanell, P. (2002, July). *The phenomenon of telecommuting and changing organizations: An organizational culture examination.* Paper presented at the annual conference of the International Communication Association, Seoul, Korea.

IDC. (2002, July 1). U.S. mobile workforce to grow twice as fast as general workforce through 2006, says IDC [Press release]. Retrieved February 9, 2003, from http://www.idc.com/getdoc.jhtml? containerId=pr2002_06_06_104004

International Facility Management Association & Haworth, Inc. (1995). *Alternative officing research and workplace strategies.* Houston, TX: IFMA.

Jackson, P., & van der Wielen, J. (1998). Introduction: Actors, approaches, and agendas: From telecommuting to the virtual organisation. In P. Jackson & J. van der Wielen (Eds.), *Teleworking: International perspectives from telecommuting to the virtual organisation* (pp. 1–17). London: Routledge.

Johnson, M. (1997). *Teleworking . . . in brief.* Oxford, UK: Butterworth-Heinemann.

Kaplan, K. (1996, July 29). For workers, telecommuting hits home. *Los Angeles Times,* p. D7.

Katz, A. (1987). The management, control, and evaluation of a telecommuting project: A case study. *Information and Management, 13,* 179–190.

Kling, R. (1996). Hopes and horrors: Technology utopianism and anti-utopianism in narratives of computerization. In R. Kling (Ed.), *Computerization and controversy: Value conflicts and social choices* (2nd ed.). New York: Academic Press.

Kompast, M., & Wagner, I. (1998). Telework: Managing spatial, temporal and cultural boundaries. In P. Jackson & J. van der Wielen (Eds.), *Teleworking: International perspectives from telecommuting to the virtual organisation* (pp. 95–117). London: Routledge.

Kramarae, C. (1995). A backstage critique of virtual reality. In S. Jones (Ed.), *CyberSociety: Computer-mediated communication and community* (pp. 36–56). Thousand Oaks, CA: Sage.

Kraut, R. (1987). Predicting the use of technology: The case of telework. In R. Kraut (Ed.), *Technology and the transformation of white-collar work.* Hillsdale, NJ: Erlbaum.

Kraut, R. (1988). Homework: What it is and who does it. In K. Christensen (Ed.), *The new era of home-based work: Directions and policies.* Boulder, CO: Westview Press.

Kraut, R., Steinfield, C., Chan, A., Butler, B., & Hoag, A. (1998). Coordination and virtualization: The role of electronic networks and personal relationships. *Journal of Computer-Mediated Communication, 3*(4) Online. Available: http://www.ascusc.org/jcmc/vol3/issue4/kraut.html

Kunda, G. (1992). *Engineering culture: Control and commitment in a high-technology corporation.* Philadelphia: Temple Press.

Kurland, N., & Egan, T. (1999, July/August). Telecommuting: Justice and control in the virtual organization. *Organizational Science, 10*(4), 500–513.

La Salle Partners & IFMA. (1998). *Alternative workplace study.* Houston, TX: IFMA.

Lea, M., & Spears, R. (1995). Love at first byte. In J. Wood & S. Duck (Eds.), *Understudied relationships* (pp. 197–264). Thousand Oaks, CA: Sage.

Lievrouw, L. A., & Livingstone, S. (2002). *The handbook of new media: Social shaping and consequences of ICTs.* Thousand Oaks, CA: Sage.

Lyall, S. (1997, November 16). It's his half-year to wash the dishes: How one couple squares 2 careers. *The New York Times,* sec. 3, pp. 1, 10.

MacKenzie, D., & Wajcman, J. (1985). Introductory essay and general issues. In D. MacKenzie & J. Wajcman (Eds.), *The social shaping of technology: How the refrigerator got its hum.* Philadelphia: Open University Press.

Malone, T., & Rockart, J. (1991, September). Computers, networks and the corporation. *Scientific American, 265*(3), 128–136.

Mankin, D., Cohen, S., & Bikson, T. (1996). *Teams and technology: Fulfilling the promise of the new organization.* Boston: Harvard Business School Press.

Manley, J., & Tolbert, C. (1997, August). *What, if anything, are telecommuters? Communication technology, labor markets and organizational control.* Paper presented at the ASA annual meeting, Toronto, Ontario, Canada.

Markus, M. L. (1996). Finding a happy medium: Explaining the negative effects of electronic communication on social life at work. In R. Kling (Ed.), *Computerization and controversy: Value conflicts and social choices* (2nd Ed.). New York: Academic Press. (Reprinted from *ACM Transactions on Information Systems, 12*(2), April 1994)

Martin, J. (1992). *Cultures in organizations: Three perspectives.* New York: Oxford University Press.

Martin, J., Feldman, M., Hatch, M. J., & Sitkin, S. (1983). The uniqueness paradox in organizational stories. *Administrative Science Quarterly, 28,* 438–453.

McGrath, P., & Houlihan, M. (1998). Conceptualising telework: Modern or postmodern? In P. Jackson & J. van der Wielen (Eds.), *Teleworking: International perspectives from telecommuting to the virtual organisation* (pp. 56–73). London: Routledge.

McLaughlin, M. L., Osborne, K. K., & Ellison, N. B. (1997). Virtual community in a telepresence environment. In S. Jones (Ed.), *Virtual* culture: Identity and communication in cybersociety (pp. 146–168). Thousand Oaks, CA: Sage.

Mirchandani, K. (1998a). No longer a struggle? Teleworkers' reconstruction of the work–non-work boundary. In P. Jackson & J. van der Wielen (Eds.), Teleworking: International perspectives from telecommuting to the virtual organisation (pp. 118–135). London: Routledge.

Mirchandani, K. (1998b). "The best of both worlds" and "Cutting my own throat": Contradictory images of home-based work. Paper presented at the annual meeting of the American Sociological Association, San Francisco, CA.

Mogelonsky, M. (1995, June). Myths of telecommuting. American Demographics, 17(6), 15–16.

Mokhtarian, P. (1991a). Defining telecommuting. Transportation Research Record, 1305, 273–281.

Mokhtarian, P. (1991b). Telecommuting and travel: State of the practice, state of the art. Transportation, 18, 319–342.

Mumby, D. K. (1998). Organizing men: Power, discourse, and the social construction of masculinity(s) in the workplace. Communication Theory, 8, 164–182.

National Research Council. (1994). Research recommendations to facilitate distributed work. Washington, DC: National Academy Press.

Nielsen/NetRatings. (2003, January 15). Broadband access grows 59 percent, while narrowband use declines. New York: Author.

Nilles, J. (1991). Telecommuting and urban sprawl: Mitigator or inciter? Transportation, 18, 411–432.

Nilles, J. (1997). Telework: Enabling distributed organizations: Implications for IT managers. Information Systems Management, 14(4), 7–14.

Nilles, J. (1998). Managing telework: Strategies for managing the virtual workforce. New York: Wiley.

Nilles, J., Carlson, F. R., Gray, P., & Hanneman, G. (1976). The telecommunications-transportation tradeoff: Options for tomorrow. New York: Wiley.

Nippert-Eng, C. (1996). Home and work: Negotiating boundaries through everyday life. Chicago: University of Chicago Press.

Nohria, N., & Berkley, J. D. (1994). The virtual organization: Bureaucracy, technology, and the implosion of control. In C. Heckscher & A. Donnellon (Eds.), The post-bureaucratic organization (pp. 108–128). Thousand Oaks, CA: Sage.

Nonaka, I. (1994). A dynamic theory of organizational knowledge creation. Organization Science, 5, 14–37.

Olson, M. (1983, March). Remote office work: Changing work patterns in space and time. Communications of the ACM, 26(3), 182–187.

Olson, M. H. (1987). Telework: Practical experience and future prospects. In R. Kraut (Ed.), Technology and the transformation of white-collar work (pp. 135–152). Hillsdale, NJ: Erlbaum.

Olson, M. H. (1988a). Corporate culture and the homeworker. In K. Christensen (Ed.), *The new era of home-based work: Directions and policies.* Boulder, CO: Westview Press.

Olson, M. H. (1988b). Organizational barriers to telework. In W. B. Korte, S. Robinson, & W. J. Steinle (Eds.), *Telework: Present situation and future development of a new form of work organisation* (pp. 77–100). Amsterdam: Elsevier Science Publishers B.V.

Olson, M. H. (1989, October). Work at home for computer professionals: Current attitudes and future prospects. *ACM Transactions on Office Information Systems, 7*(4), 317–338.

Olson, M. H., & Primps, S. B. (1990). Working at home with computers. In M. D. Ermann, M. Williams, & C. Gutierrez (Eds.), *Computers, ethics and society.* New York: Oxford University Press. (Reprinted from *JSI, 40*(3), 1984)

Orlikowski, W. (1992). The duality of technology: Rethinking the concept of technology in organizations. *Organization Science, 3*, 398–427.

Orlikowski, W. (1996). Improvising organizational transformation over time: A situated change perspective. *Information Systems Research, 7*(1), 63–92.

Pancucci, D. (1995, April). Remote control. *Management Today,* 78–80.

Park, G. S., Nilles, J. M., & Baer, W. S. (1996). *Trends and factors influencing telecommuting in Southern California.* Santa Monica, CA: RAND.

Parks, M. R., & Floyd, K. (1996). Making friends in cyberspace. *Journal of Communication, 46*(1), 80–97.

Parliamentary Office of Science and Technology. (1995, June). *Working at a distance: UK teleworking and its implications.* London: Author.

Perin, C. (1991). The moral fabric of the office: Panopticon discourse and schedule flexibility. In P. Tolbert & S. Barley (Eds.), *Research in the sociology of organizations* (vol. 8, pp. 243–270). Greenwich, CT: JAI Press.

Pool, I. (1990). *Technologies without boundaries: On telecommunications in a global age* (E. Noam, Ed.). Cambridge, MA: Harvard University Press.

Pratt, J. (1984). Home teleworking: A study of its pioneers. *Technological Forecasting and Social Change, 25*, 1–14.

PS Enterprises. (1995). *On telecommuting: A PS Enterprises research paper.* Retrieved January 30, 2003, from http://www.psenterprises.com/telecom.htm

Qvortrup, L. (1998). From telework to networking: Definitions and trends. In P. Jackson & J. van der Wielen (Eds.), *Teleworking: International perspectives from telecommuting to the virtual organisation* (pp. 21–39). London: Routledge.

Raghuram, S. (1996). Knowledge creation in the telework context. *International Journal of Technology Management, 11*, 859–870.

Rainie, L. (2002, January 1). *Women surpass men as online shoppers during the holidays.* Pew Internet & American Life Project. Retrieved February 9, 2003, from http://www.pewinternet.org/reports/pdfs/PIP_Holiday_2001_Report.pdf

Ramsower, R. M. (1985). *Telecommuting: The organizational and behavioral effects of working at home.* Ann Arbor, MI: UMI Research Press.

Rawlins, W. K. (1998). Theorizing public and private domains and practices of communication: Introductory concerns. *Communication Theory, 8*(4), 369–380.

Reinsch, N. L. (1997). Relationships between telecommuting workers and their managers: An exploratory study. *The Journal of Business Communication, 34,* 343–367.

Reynolds, T., & Brusseau, D. (1998). *Cyberlane commuter.* South Pasadena, CA: iLAN Systems.

Rheingold, H. (1993). *The virtual community: Homesteading on the electronic frontier.* Reading, MA: Addison-Wesley.

Rheingold, H. (2002). *Smart mobs: The next social revolution.* Cambridge, MA: Basic Books.

Rice, R. (1992). Contexts of research of organizational computer-mediated communication: A recursive review. In M. Lea (Ed.), *Contexts of computer-mediated communication.* London: Harvester-Wheatsheaf.

Rice, R. (1993). Media appropriateness: Using social presence theory to compare traditional and new organizational media. *Human Communication Research, 19*(4), 451–484.

Rice, R., & Love, G. (1987). Electronic emotion: Socioemotional content in a computer-mediated communication network. *Communication Research, 14*(1), 85–108.

Robinson, J., & Godbey, G. (1997). *Time for life: The surprising ways Americans use their time.* University Park: Pennsylvania State University Press.

Rose, F. (1997, September 2). Work week: Office "hoteling" isn't as inn as futurists once thought. *Wall Street Journal,* p. A1.

Salomon, I., & Salomon, M. (1984). Telecommuting: The employee's perspective. *Technological Forecasting and Social Change, 25,* 15–28.

Sato, K., & Spinks, W. (1998). Telework and crisis management in Japan. In P. Jackson & J. van der Wielen (Eds.), *Teleworking: International perspectives from telecommuting to the virtual organisation* (pp. 233–244). London: Routledge.

Schein, E. H. (1985). *Organizational culture and leadership: A dynamic view.* San Francisco: Jossey-Bass.

Schein, E. H. (1991). The role of the founder in the creation of organizational culture. In P. Frost, L. Moore, C. Lundberg, M. Louis, & J. Martin (Eds.), *Reframing organizational culture* (pp. 243–253). Newbury Park, CA: Sage.

Schmitz, J., & Fulk, J. (1991). Organizational colleagues, media richness, and electronic mail: A test of the social influence model of technology use. *Communication Research, 18*(4), 487–523.

Schor, J. (1991). *The overworked American: The unexpected decline of leisure.* New York: Basic Books.

Scott, C. R., & Timmerman, C. E. (1999). Communication technology use and multiple workplace identifications among organizational teleworkers with varied degrees of virtuality. *IEEE Transactions on Professional Communication, 42,* 240–260.

Sellen, A. J., & Harper, R. H. (2001). *The myth of the paperless office.* Cambridge, MA: MIT Press.

Shafizadeh, K., Niemeier, D., Mokhtarian, P., & Salomon, I. (1997, September 21–25). *The costs and benefits of telecommuting: An evaluation of macro-scale literature.* Paper presented at the 8th Meeting of the International Association for Travel Behaviour Research, Austin, TX.

Shamir, B. (1992). Home: The perfect workplace? In S. Zedeck (Ed.), *Work, families, and organizations* (pp. 272–311). San Francisco: Jossey-Bass.

Shamir, B., & Salomon, I. (1985). Work-at-home and the quality of working life. *Academy of Management Review, 10*(3) 455–464.

Shellenbarger, S. (1997a, July 30). Do we work more or not? Either way, we feel frazzled. *Wall Street Journal,* p. B1.

Shellenbarger, S. (1997b, August 20). Madison Avenue needs to alter image of '90s telecommuters. *Wall Street Journal,* p. B1.

Shellenbarger, S. (2002, January 23). Workers get creative finding places to sit and "telework." *Wall Street Journal.* Retrieved November 16, 2002, from http://online.wsj.com/ article/0,,SB1011732372214631520-search,00.html? collection=wsjie%2Farchive&vql_string=telework%3Cin%3E% 28article%2Dbody%29

Short, J., Williams, E., & Christie, B. (1976). *The social psychology of telecommunications.* London: Wiley.

Sias, P., & Cahill, D. (1998). From coworkers to friends: The development of peer friendships in the workplace. *Western Journal of Communication, 62*(3), 273–299.

Silverstone, R. (1994). *Television and everyday life.* London: Routledge.

Silverstone, R. (1996). Future imperfect: Information and communication technologies in everyday life. In W. Dutton (Ed.), *Information and communication technologies: Visions and realities.* Oxford, UK: Oxford University Press.

Smircich, L., & Calas, M. B. (1987). Organizational culture: A critical assessment. In F. M. Jablin, L. L. Putnam, K. H. Roberts, & L. W. Porter (Eds.), *Handbook of organizational communication: An interdisciplinary perspective* (pp. 228–263). Newbury Park, CA: Sage.

Smith, R. (1996, November). *Home alone: An ethnography of communicative behavior enacted by telecommuters.* Paper presented at the annual meeting of the Speech Communication Association, San Diego, CA.

Sproull, L., & Kiesler, K. (1991). Computers, networks and work. *Scientific American, 235*(3), 116–123.

Steinle, W. J. (1988). Telework: Opening remarks on an open debate. In W. B. Korte, S. Robinson, & W. J. Steinle (Eds.), *Telework: Present situation and future development of a new form of work organization* (pp. 7–19). Amsterdam: Elsevier Science Publishers B.V.

Stohl, C. (1995). *Organizational communication: Connectedness in action.* Thousand Oaks, CA: Sage.

Switzer, T. (1997). *Telecommuters, the workforce of the twenty-first century: An annotated bibliography.* Lanham, MD: Scarecrow Press.

Symantec. (n.d.). *pcTelecommute.* Retrieved November 9, 1998, from http://www.symantec.com/pctelecommute/fs_pct.html

Takahashi, D. (1996, November 18). Road warrior. *Wall Street Journal,* p. R27.

Talbot, M. (1997, October 20 & 27). Dial-a-wife. *The New Yorker,* pp. 196–208.

Toffler, A. (1980). *The third wave.* New York: Morrow.

Trevino, L. K., Daft, R. L., & Lengel, R. H. (1990). Understanding managers' media choices: A symbolic interactionist perspective. In J. Fulk & C. Steinfield (Eds.), *Organizations and communication technology* (pp. 71–94). Newbury Park, CA: Sage.

Turkle, S. (1995). *Life on the screen: Identity in the age of the Internet.* New York: Touchstone.

U.S. Department of Labor. (1998). *Work at home in 1997.* Online. Available: http://stats.bls.gov/news.release/homey.toc.htm

Van Maanen, J. (1991). The smile factory: Work at Disneyland. In P. Frost, L. Moore, M. L. Louis, C. Lundberg, & J. Martin (Eds.), *Reframing organizational culture* (pp. 58–76). Beverly Hills, CA: Sage.

Walther, J. (1992). Interpersonal effects in computer-mediated interaction: A relational perspective. *Communication Research, 19*(1), 52–90.

Walther, J. (1996). Computer-mediated communication: Impersonal, interpersonal and hyperpersonal interaction. *Communication Research, 23*(4), 3–43.

Walther, J. B., Anderson, J. F., & Park, D. W. (1994). Interpersonal effects in computer-mediated interaction: A meta-analysis of social and antisocial communication. *Communication Research, 21*(4), 460–487.

Webster, J. (1996). Revolution in the office? Implications for women's paid work. In W. Dutton (Ed.), *Information and communication technologies: Visions and realities.* Oxford, UK: Oxford University Press.

Weick, K. E. (1979). *The social psychology of organizing* (2nd ed.). New York: McGraw-Hill.

Wells, S. (1997, August 17). For stay-home workers, speed bumps on the telecommute. *New York Times,* sec. 3, p. 1.

Westfall, R. D. (1997). The telecommuting paradox. *Information Systems Management, 14*(4), 15–18.

Westfall, R. D. (1998). The microeconomics of remote work. In M. Igbaria & M. Tan (Eds.), *The virtual workplace* (pp. 218–255). Hershey, PA: Idea Group.
Wiesenfeld, B., Raghuram, S., & Garud, R. (1998). Communication
  patterns as determinants of organizational identification in a virtual organization. *Journal of Computer-Mediated Communication*
  3(4). Retrieved September 9, 2002, from http://www.ascusc.
  org/jcmc/vol3/issue4/wiesenfeld.html
Wilcot, W. (1995). *Relational communication.* New York: McGraw-Hill.
Wilgoren, J. (1998, September 7). With labor day comes more labor, less
  play. *Los Angeles Times.* Retrieved September 8, 1998, from
  http://www.latimes.com/HOME/NEWS/FRONT/t000081371.ht
  ml
Winner, L. (1994). Three paradoxes of the information age. In G. Ben-
  der & T. Druckrey (Eds.), *Cultures on the brink* (pp. 90–98). Seat-
  tle, WA: Bay Press.
Woolgar, S. (1996). Technologies as cultural artifacts. In W. Dutton
  (Ed.), *Information and communication technologies: Visions and*
  realities. Oxford, UK: Oxford University Press.
Wright, P., & Oldford, A. (1993). Telecommuting and employee effec-
  tiveness: Career and managerial issues. *International Journal of*
  Career Management, 5(1),4–9.
Yin, R. (1984). *Case study research: Design and methods.* Beverly Hills,
  CA: Sage.
Zedeck, S. (1992). Introduction: Exploring the domain of work and
  family concerns. In S. Zedeck (Ed.), *Work, families, and organi-*
  zations (pp. 1–32). San Francisco: Jossey-Bass.
Zedeck, S., & Mosier, K. (1990). Work in the family and employing
  organization. *American Psychologist, 45*(2), 240–251.
Zimmerman, J. (1990). Some effects of the new technology on women.
  In M. D. Ermann, M. Williams, & C. Gutierrez (Eds.), *Computers,*
  ethics and society. New York: Oxford University Press. (Reprinted
  from *Once Upon the Future,* pp. 29–32, 55–61, 66–71, by Jan
  Zimmerman, 1986, Pandora Press in association with Methuen)
Zuboff, S. (1988). *In the age of the smart machine: The future of power*
  and work. New York: Basic Books.

Index

About the Author

NICOLE B. ELLISON is an assistant professor in the Department of Telecommunication, Information Studies and Media at Michigan State University. Previously, she was a faculty member at California State University, Stanislaus, and a senior researcher for Sapient Corporation in San Francisco. She has published research on virtual communities, telework, and online culture in journals and as book chapters in *Virtual Culture* and *Doing Internet Research*.